Passing the

Numeracy Skills Test

Passing the

Numeracy Skills Test

6th Edition

Mark Patmore

 SAGE | LearningMatters

Los Angeles | London | New Delhi
Singapore | Washington DC

Learning Matters
An imprint of SAGE Publications Ltd
1 Oliver's Yard
55 City Road
London EC1Y 1SP

SAGE Publications Inc.
2455 Teller Road
Thousand Oaks, California 91320

SAGE Publications India Pvt Ltd
B 1/I 1 Mohan Cooperative Industrial Area
Mathura Road
New Delhi 110 044

SAGE Publications Asia-Pacific Pte Ltd
3 Church Street
#10-04 Samsung Hub
Singapore 049483

Editor: Amy Thornton
Development editor: Geoff Barker
Production controller: Chris Marke
Project management: Deer Park Productions,
Tavistock, Devon
Marketing manager: Lorna Patkai
Cover design: Wendy Scott
Typeset by: C&M Digitals (P) Ltd, Chennai, India
Printed and bound by CPI Group (UK) Ltd,
Croydon, CR0 4YY

First published in 2000 by Learning Matters Ltd

Second edition published in 2001. Reprinted in 2001
(twice) and 2002 (twice). Third edition published
in 2003. Reprinted in 2004 (twice), 2005 (twice)
and 2006 (twice). Fourth edition published in 2008.
Reprinted in 2009 (twice). Fifth edition published in
2012. Reprinted in 2013. Revised fifth edition printed
in 2013. Reprinted in 2013. Sixth edition published
in 2015.

Library of Congress Control Number: 2014953634

British Library Cataloguing in Publication data

A catalogue record for this book is available from
the British Library.

ISBN 978-1-4739-1174-1
ISBN 978-1-4739-1175-8 (pbk)

At SAGE we take sustainability seriously. Most of our products are printed in the UK using FSC papers and boards.
When we print overseas we ensure sustainable papers are used as measured by the Egmont grading system.
We undertake an annual audit to monitor our sustainability.

Contents

Acknowledgements

The glossary is reproduced courtesy of the Standards Testing Agency. Permission to reproduce such copyright material does not extend to any material which is identified as being the copyright of a third party or any photographs. Authorisation to reproduce such material would need to be obtained from the copyright holders.

About the author

Mark Patmore is a former senior lecturer in mathematical education at the School of Education at Nottingham Trent University. He is currently working in teacher education with other universities and training providers and also provides CPD for teachers of mathematics. After some years as a numeracy consultant for the Teacher Training Agency, Mark was for several years one of the writers for the numeracy skills tests and then a member of the Test Review Group managed by Alpha*Plus* Consultancy which monitored the writing of the tests.

Mark is Chief Examiner for the Cambridge Award in Mathematics and is involved with assessing and verifying a range of educational qualifications. He is the author or co-author of a number of publications for both GCSE and Key Stage 3 Mathematics.

Series introduction

The QTS skills tests

All applicants for initial teacher training (ITT) courses which began in September 2014, or will begin in September 2015 and beyond, are required to have passed the qualified teacher status (QTS) skills tests in both numeracy and literacy before the start of their course.

This applies to those intending to follow an employment-based route into teaching, such as the School Direct programme, as well as those intending to take the PGCE route and includes applicants for the Assessment Only route.

Note 1: Applicants will need to take proof of application to ITT with them on the day(s) of their test(s).

Note 2: Existing trainees on courses that started before 1 July 2013 still need to pass the skills tests in order to achieve QTS.

The tests cover skills in:

- numeracy;
- literacy.

Applicants will be allowed three attempts to pass the numeracy skills test and three attempts to pass the literacy skills test. The first attempt is free but each of the two resits is charged currently at £19.25. Applicants who fail three attempts are 'barred' from making further attempts for a period of two years.

The tests will demonstrate that a trainee can apply these skills to the degree necessary for their use in day-to-day work in a school, rather than the subject knowledge required for teaching. The tests are taken online by booking a time at a specified centre, are marked instantly and the result, along with feedback on that result, will be given to applicants before they leave the centre.

There is more information about the skills tests and the specified centres on the following website: www.education.gov.uk/sta/professional.

Titles in this series

This series of books is designed to help you become familiar with the skills you will need to pass the tests and to practise questions on each of the topic areas to be tested.

Passing the Numeracy Skills Test (sixth edition)
Mark Patmore
ISBN 978 1 4739 1175 8 (pbk)
ISBN 978 1 4739 1174 1 (hbk)

Passing the Literacy Skills Test (fourth edition)
Jim Johnson and Bruce Bond
ISBN 978 1 4739 1343 1 (pbk)
ISBN 978 1 4739 1342 4 (hbk)

Introduction

Introduction to the test

The numeracy skills test is a computerised test, which is divided into two sections:

- section 1 for the mental arithmetic questions;
- section 2 for the written questions known as 'on-screen' questions.

The **mental arithmetic** section is an audio test heard through headphones. Calculators are not allowed, but noting numbers and jotting down working will be permitted. (You will be issued with a wipe-clean board and a pen to help with this.) There are 12 questions in this section. Note: this section must be answered first; each question has a fixed time in which you must answer (18 seconds); you cannot return to a question if you later wish to change your answer. Questions will be asked to test your ability to carry out mental calculations using fractions, percentages, measurement, conversions and time (see the detailed content list on page 5).

The **'on-screen'** questions: there are 16 written questions in this section. Seven questions are focused on *interpreting* and using written data and nine are focused on *solving* written arithmetic problems. Questions and answers will be in one of the following forms:

- multiple-choice questions where you will choose the single correct response from a fixed number of alternative answers;
- multiple-response questions where you choose single or multiple correct statements from a fixed number of given statements;
- questions that require a single answer;
- questions where you will select the answer by pointing and clicking on the correct point in a table, chart or graph (to change an answer click on an alternative point);
- questions where you will select your answer from a number of alternative answers and place the answer into the answer box provide (to change an answer drag it back to its original position and choose another).

In this part of the test you can use the 'on-screen' calculator. You answer questions using the mouse and the keyboard and you can move between questions by using the 'next' and 'previous' buttons. You can return to questions either by using the 'flag' button and then the 'review' button or by waiting until the end of the test when you will have the option of reviewing all the questions – provided there is time!

Chapter 3 provides guidance, examples and questions on *solving* written arithmetic problems. Your ability to use general everyday arithmetic correctly using, for example, time, money, ratio and proportion, fractions, decimals and percentages, distance and area, conversions between currencies, simple formulae and averages, including mean, median, mode and range, is assessed.

Chapter 4 provides guidance, examples and questions on *interpreting* and using written data. Your ability to identify trends correctly, to make comparisons and draw conclusions, and interpret charts and tables correctly is assessed.

Time for the test

The time limit for the whole test is approximately 48 minutes – at the end of which the test will shut down automatically.

The contexts for the questions

One of the aims of the numeracy skills test is to ensure that teachers have the skills and understanding necessary to analyse the sort of data that is now in schools. Consequently most questions will be set within contexts such as:

- national test data;
- target setting and school improvement data;
- pupil progress and attainment over time;
- special educational needs (SEN);
- GCSE subject choices and results.

Hints and advice

The mental arithmetic, audio section

Each mental arithmetic question is heard twice. After the first reading an answer box appears on the screen. You will have a short time – 18 seconds – to work out the answer and type it into the answer box, after which the next question will automatically appear. As mentioned earlier, you cannot move forwards or backwards between questions. At the start of the test you will hear a practice question.

- Concentrate the first time the question is read, and note down the key numbers. For example, a question could be 'In a class of 30 pupils, 24 are boys. What fraction are girls?'. You should jot down 30 and 24. The second time the question is heard, concentrate on what to do with those numbers (for example, $30 - 24 = 6$ (so there are 6 girls) then $6/30 = 1/5$).

- Start to work out the answer as soon as you have the information. You may be able to do this while you hear the second reading of the question.

- If you cannot answer a question don't worry or panic – enter a likely answer, then forget it. Remember, you don't need to get every single question right.

- Note that you don't have to worry about units, i.e. £ or € or cm, for example. The units will appear in the answer box.

- Listen carefully to what the question requires in the answer. For example, a question could ask for a time 'using the 24-hour clock', or an answer 'to the nearest whole number', or 'to two decimal places'. (There are notes on this in Chapter 3.)

- Fractions need to be entered in the lowest terms. For example, 6/8 should be entered as 3/4 and 7/28 should be entered as 1/4.

- Practise using mental strategies. For example, purchasing five books that cost £5.99 can be worked out by multiplying 5 x £6 (£30) and subtracting 5 x lp (5p) to give the answer of £29.95.

- Remember the link between fractions and percentages – see Chapter 1.

The on-screen questions

- Try not to spend more than two minutes on any one question and keep an eye on the time remaining. If you think you are exceeding the time then move on – you can always return to any you still need to complete at the end of the test and insert an answer. Try not to leave any answers blank at the end of the test.

- Read each question carefully. For example, a question may ask for the percentage of pupils who achieved level 4 and above. Don't just look at those who gained level 4; the question included the words 'and above', so you need to include those who achieved 'above', i.e. achieved level 5, level 6, and so on.

- Check that you are giving the correct information in the answer. A table may give you details of the number of marks a pupil achieved but the question may be asking for a percentage score.

The on-screen calculator

When the mental arithmetic section of the test is finished, a basic four-function calculator will be available on the screen for you to use for the rest of the test. No other calculators can be used. You can move the calculator around the screen using the mouse. The on-screen calculator works through the mouse and through the number pad on the keyboard. If you wish to use the number pad you must ensure that the number lock key 'Num Lock' is activated.

Notes on using the on-screen calculator

- To cancel an operation, press CE .

- Always use the 'clear' button C on the calculator before beginning a new calculation.

- Always check the display of the calculator to make sure that the number shown is what you wanted.

- Check calculations and make sure that your final answer makes sense in the context of the question. For example, the number of pupils gaining level 5 in a test will not be greater than the size of the cohort or group.

Other hints

1. Rounding up and down

- Make sure that any instructions to round an answer up or down are followed – or the answer will be marked as incorrect.

- Use the context to make sure whether a decimal answer should be rounded up or down. For example, an answer of 16.4 lessons for a particular activity is clearly not appropriate and the answer would need to be rounded up to 17 lessons.

- Questions may specify that the answer should be rounded to the nearest whole number or be rounded to two decimal places. See the notes at the start of Chapter 3.

- When carrying out calculations relating to money, the answer shown on the calculator display will need to be rounded to the nearest penny (unless otherwise indicated). Hence, if calculating in pounds, round to two decimal places to show the number of pence. If 10.173 is the answer in pounds on the calculator display, rounding to the nearest penny gives £10.17.

2. Answering multi-stage questions

The calculator provided is not a scientific calculator and therefore care needs to be taken with 'mixed operations' (i.e. calculations using several function keys). It is important that the function keys are pressed in the appropriate order for the calculation. It may also be useful to note down answers to particular stages of the calculation.

It is important to remember to carry out the calculation required by the question in the following order: any calculation within brackets followed by division/multiplication followed by addition and/or subtraction. Thus, the answer to the calculation $2 + 3 \times 4$ is 14

and not 20; the answer to $\frac{18}{3+6}$ is $\frac{18}{9} = 2$; and the answer to $\frac{18}{3} + 6 = 6 + 6 = 12$. See the notes at the start of Chapter 3.

3. Dealing with fractions

Although fractions will appear in the usual format within a question (for example, $\frac{3}{4}$), to enter a fraction in an answer, use the 'forward slash' key (for example, 'one-half' would be entered as 1/2). To use the on-screen calculator to calculate with fractions then it is probably easier to deal with the fraction first, converting it into a decimal, and then multiply by this decimal. For example, to calculate $\frac{5}{8}$ of 320, first enter 5/8 = 0.625. Multiply 0.625 by 320, obtaining 200 as the answer.

How to use this book

The book is divided into six chapters.

Chapter 1: this very short chapter has been included to remind you of the basic arithmetic processes. The majority of you will be able to miss this unit out, but some may welcome a chance to revise fractions, decimals, percentages, etc.

Chapters 2–4: these cover the three 'content' areas (see above), one area per chapter.

Chapter 5: this includes a practice mental arithmetic test, and a full practice onscreen test for you to work through.

Chapter 6: this contains answers and key points for all the questions in the main chapters and for the sample tests.

In each chapter, the additional required knowledge, language and vocabulary are explained, and worked examples of the type of questions to be faced are provided together with the practice questions. The answers for these questions are given in Chapter 6, together with further advice and guidance on solutions.

Revision checklists

The following charts show in detail the coverage of the three main chapters and the practice tests. You can use the checklists in your revision to make sure that you have covered all the key content areas.

Revision checklist for Chapter 2: Mental arithmetic

Syllabus Reference	Content	Question
1a	Time – varied contexts	1, 7, 18, 21, 34, 39, 44
1b	Amounts of money – varied contexts	12, 38, 41, 43
1c/d/e	1c Proportion – answer as a fraction 1d Proportion – answer as a percentage 1e Proportion – answer as a decimal	37 27 22
1f	Fractions	16, 29, 45
1g	Decimals	32
1h	Percentages – varied contexts	2, 11, 19, 20, 24, 26, 30, 35, 42
1i/j/k	1i Measurements – distance 1j Measurements – area 1k Measurements – other	23, 36 25, 40
1l/m/n/o/p/q	1l Conversions from one currency to another 1m Conversions – from fractions to decimals 1n Conversions – from decimals to fractions 1o Conversions – from percentages to 1p Conversions – from fractions to percentages 1q Conversions – other	 15 31 4, 9, 13, 28, 33 6
1r	Combination of one or more of addition, subtraction, multiplication, division (may involve amounts of money or whole numbers)	3, 5, 8, 10, 14, 17

Revision checklist for Chapter 3: Solving written arithmetic problems

(Note: Only the main references are used; many questions will cover more than one reference.)

Syllabus Reference	Content	Question
3a	Time – varied contexts	7, 17, 23, 29, 31, 33
3b	Amounts of money	2, 57, 60(a)
3c, d, e, f	3c Proportion – answer as a fraction	14
	3d Proportion – answer as a percentage	14
	3e Proportion – answer as a decimal	14, 62(b)
	3f Ratios	3, 59, 60(b)

(Continued)

(Continued)

Syllabus Reference	Content	Question
3g	Percentages – varied contexts	4, 5, 6, 8, 9, 10, 11, 12, 13, 18, 27, 39, 42, 47, 56(a), 62(a)
3h	Fractions	19, 24, 54
3i	Decimals	41
3j, k, l, m, n	3j Measurements – distance	21, 26, 28, 30, 36
	3k Measurements – area	22
	3l Conversions – from one currency to another	2
	3m Conversions – from fractions to decimals or vice versa	14
	3n Conversions – other	15, 16, 20, 24, 38, 48, 61
3o, p, q, r, s	3o Averages – mean 3p Averages – median 3q Averages – mode	45, 58
	3r Range	35, 56(b)
	3s Averages – combination	1, 34, 44
3t	Given formulae	32, 40, 43, 46, 49, 50, 5 1, 52, 53, 55

Revision checklist for Chapter 4: Interpreting and using written data

(Note: Only the main references are used; many questions will cover more than one reference.)

Syllabus Reference	Content	Question
2a	Identify trends over time	9, 13, 17, 19, 21
2b	Make comparisons in order to draw conclusions	2, 5, 10, 11, 12, 14, 23, 24
2c	Interpret and use information	1, 3, 4, 6, 7, 8, 15, 16, 18, 20
3o	Averages	9

Revision checklist for the practice mental arithmetic test

Syllabus Reference	Content	Question
1a	Time – varied contexts	6
1b	Amounts of money – varied contexts	7, 10
1c/d/e	1c Proportion – answer as a fraction 1d Proportion – answer as a percentage 1e Proportion – answer as a decimal	
1f	Fractions	12
1g	Decimals	
1h	Percentages – varied contexts	2, 3, 5, 8
1i/j/k	1i Measurements – distance 1j Measurements – area 1k Measurements – other	

Syllabus Reference	Content	Question
1l/m/n/o/p/q	1l Conversions – from one currency to another	9
	1m Conversions – from fractions to decimals	
	1n Conversions – from decimals to fractions	
	1o conversions – from percentages to fractions	
	1p Conversions – from fractions to percentages	
	1q Conversions – other	4
1r	Combination of one or more of addition, subtraction, multiplication, division (may involve amounts of money or whole numbers)	1, 11

Revision checklist for the practice on-screen test

Syllabus Reference	Content	Question
2a	Identify trends over time	4, 9
2b	Make comparisons in order to draw conclusions	1, 8
2c	Interpret and use information	2, 6, 7
3a	Time – varied contexts	
3b	Amounts of money	3, 10, 13
3c, d, e, f	3c Proportion – answer as a fraction 3d Proportion – answer as a percentage 3e Proportion – answer as a decimal 3f Ratios	5, 14
3g	Percentages – varied contexts	15, 16
3h	Fractions	
3i	Decimals	
3j, k, l, m, n	3j Measurements – distance 3k Measurements – area 3l Conversions – from one currency to another 3m Conversions – from fractions to decimals or vice versa 3n Conversions - other	
3o, p, q, r, s	3o Averages – mean 3p Averages – median 3q Averages – mode 3r Range 3s Averages-combination	
3t	Given formulae	9, 11

1 | Key knowledge

Fractions, decimals and percentages

You must remember decimals and place value:

hundreds	tens	ones	.	tenths	hundredths
4	3	5	•	2	7

4 hundreds + 3 tens + 5 ones + 2 tenths + 7 hundredths

$$= 400 + 30 + 5 + \frac{2}{10} + \frac{7}{100}$$

$$= 435.27$$

Take care when adding or subtracting decimals to line up the decimal points. Remember, too, when multiplying decimals by 10 that all the digits move one place to the left, so 435.27 × 10 becomes 4352.7 (the rule you will probably remember is 'move the decimal point one place to the right'); and when dividing by 100, the digits move two places to the right, so 4352.7 ÷ 100 becomes 43.527 (similarly the rule you may remember is 'move the decimal point two places to the left').

When multiplying two decimals the method you may remember is to *ignore* the decimal points, do the multiplication and then count up the number of decimal figures in the question numbers. The total will give the number of decimal figures in the answer number, so that 0.4 × 0.5 is calculated as 4 × 5 = 20; there are 2 decimal figures in the question numbers (0.4 and 0.5) so there are 2 in the answer. Therefore, the answer is 0.20. It would be better to think of this calculation as follows:

$$0.4 \times 0.5 = \frac{4}{10} \times \frac{5}{10} = \frac{20}{100} = 0.2$$

You must remember how to work with fractions. There are several ways of 'looking' at a fraction, for example: $\frac{3}{4}$ = 3 parts out of 4; or 3 divided by 4 or 3 shared by 4 = 3 ÷ 4 = 0.75; or three lots of a quarter = $3 \times \frac{1}{4}$; or a quarter of 3 = $\frac{1}{4} \times 3$.

One way to calculate, say, $\frac{2}{5}$ of £20 is: find a fifth, £20 ÷ 5 = £4 then multiply this by 2 = £8. Another way is to change the fraction into a decimal:

$$\frac{2}{5} = 2 \div 5 = 0.4, \text{ then multiply } 0.4 \times £20 = £8.$$

You will need to know how to simplify a fraction by dividing both the numerator and the denominator by the same factor.

Example

$\frac{12}{28} = \frac{3}{7}$ dividing the numerator and the denominator by 4

or $\frac{54}{72} = \frac{27}{36} = \frac{9}{12} = \frac{3}{4}$ dividing top and bottom by 2 then by 3 and then by 3 again.

You must remember that percentages are fractions with denominators of 100 (per cent means per 100). For example, 5% represents $\frac{5}{100}$, 75% represents $\frac{75}{100}$. You can convert percentages to decimals by dividing by 100, so 5% = $\frac{5}{100}$ = 0.05, and 75% = $\frac{75}{100}$ = 0.75.

To change a fraction into a percentage first change it into a decimal and then multiply by 100.

Example

$\frac{3}{8}$ as a percentage is $3 \div 8 = 0.375, 0.375 \times 100 = 37.5\%$

To find the percentage of a quantity, change the % into a decimal and then multiply the result by the quantity.

Example

To find 30% of 50 first change 30% into a decimal (= 0.3) and then multiply by 50 giving 0.3 × 50 = 15

or find 10% of 50 = $\frac{1}{10}$ × 50 = 5 so 30% = 3 × 10% = 3 × 5 = 15

You need to be able to calculate percentages in problems such as 'what is 14 marks out of 25 marks as a percentage?'

Example

Either find 14 out of 25 as a fraction and then multiply by 100 giving is $\frac{14}{25} = \frac{14}{25}$ × 100= 14 × 4 = 56%

or use equivalent fractions: $\frac{14}{25} = \frac{56}{100}$ (multiplying numerator and denominator by 4 to get a denominator of 100)

= 56%

Example

Percentages are useful for comparisons:

In a test Richard got 40 right out of 80, Sarah got 45% and Paul managed to get $\frac{5}{8}$ correct. Who did best and who did worst in the test?

Richard got 50%; Paul got $\frac{5}{8} \times \frac{100}{1} = 62.5\%$ So Sarah did the worst and Paul did the best.

Here are some common fractions, decimals and percentages.

You should learn these.

1%	$\frac{1}{100}$	0.01	(divide by 100)
5%	$\frac{1}{20}$	0.05	(divide by 20)
10%	$\frac{1}{10}$	0.1	(divide by 10)
$12\frac{1}{2}\%$	$\frac{1}{8}$	0.125	(divide by 8)
20%	$\frac{1}{5}$	0.2	(divide by 5)
25%	$\frac{1}{4}$	0.25	(divide by 4)
50%	$\frac{1}{2}$	0.5	(divide by 2)
75%	$\frac{3}{4}$	0.75	(divide by 4, multiply by 3)

Questions

1. Calculate these totals without using a calculator:

    (a) 1.8 + 2.0 + 0.5   (b) 0.4 + 0.04 + 4   (c) 2.1 + 0.09 + 7 + 0.9

    (d) 2.8 + 3.2 − 0.6   (e) 0.04 + 1.04 + 0.4   (f) 2.01 + 0.09 + 7 + 0.09

2. Calculate these without using a calculator:

    (a) 1.4 × 30   (b) 0.5 × 0.7   (c) 0.4 × 5

3. Write these percentages as fractions in their simplest form:

    (a) 2%   (b) 25%   (c) 85%   (d) 12.5%   (e) 47%

4. Write these fractions as percentages:

   (a) $\frac{3}{8}$ (b) $\frac{13}{25}$ (c) $\frac{12}{40}$ (d) $\frac{36}{60}$

5. Work these out:

   (a) 25% of £40   (b) 75% of £20   (c) 12% of 50   (d) 20% of 45

6. Simplify these fractions, writing them in their lowest terms:

   (a) $\frac{24}{36}$ (b) $\frac{18}{30}$ (c) $\frac{30}{75}$ (d) $\frac{75}{100}$

7. Which is largest?

   $\frac{90}{150}, \frac{39}{60}, \frac{61}{100}$

Mean, median, mode and range

The *mean* is the average most people give if asked for an average – the mean is found by adding up all the values in the list and dividing this total by the number of values.

The *median* is the middle value when all the values in the list are put in size order. If there are two 'middle' values the median is the mean of these two.

The *mode* is the most common value.

The *range* is the difference between the highest value and the lowest value.

Example

This example should illustrate each of the four calculations.

The children in Class 6 gained the following marks in a test:

Boys	45	46	48	60	42	53	47	51
	54	54	49	48	47	53	48	45
Girls	45	47	47	55	46	53	54	63
	48	50	46	51	48	48		

Work out the mean, median, mode and range for the boys and girls and compare the distributions of the marks.

(Continued)

11

(Continued)

The calculation for the boys:

$$Mean: \frac{42+45+45+46+47+47+48+48+48+49+51+53+53+54+54+60}{16}$$

= 49 (to the nearest whole number)

Median: there are 16 values, so the median is midway between the 8th and 9th values

$$= \frac{48+48}{2} = 48$$

The *mode* is 48.

The *range* is 60 − 42 = 18.

Question

8. Now work out the values for the girls. Then compare the distributions.

2 | Mental arithmetic

Notes

The mathematics required in this part of the test should usually be straightforward. The content and skills likely to be tested are listed in the Introduction (see page 5). Look back at this to remind yourself.

Key point

When you are taking the test, listen for, and jot down, numbers that may give short cuts or ease the calculations, such as those that allow doubling and halving. For example, multiply by 100 then divide by 2 if you need to multiply by 50, or multiply by 100 and divide by 4 if you are multiplying by 25. To calculate percentages, first find 10% by dividing by 10 then double for 20% or divide by 2 for 5% and so on. Look back at the hints in the Introduction.

Remember

- Calculators are not allowed.
- Questions will be read out twice. When answering the questions in this section, ask someone to read each question out to you and then, without a pause, read out the question again.
- There should then be a pause to allow you to record the answer before the next question is read out. The pause should be 18 seconds long.

Hint

You might find it helpful to ask someone to read out these practice questions. They will need to read them out at a sensible speed, as if they were reading a story to children. Remind them that each question should be read out twice and that they should then pause for 18 seconds, before reading out the next question. Numbers in these questions are in words, rather than using digits, to emphasise that they are spoken.

Questions

1. As part of a two and a quarter hour tennis training session, pupils received specialist coaching for one hour and twenty minutes. How many minutes of the training session remained?

(Continued)

(Continued)

2. A test has forty questions, each worth one mark. The pass mark was seventy per cent. How many questions had to be answered correctly to pass the test?

3. Dining tables seat six children. How many tables are needed to seat one hundred children?

4. Three classes of twenty-eight pupils took the end of Key Stage 2 mathematics test. Sixty-three pupils gained a level 5 result. What percentage is this?

5. A coach holds fifty-two passengers. How many coaches will be needed for a school party of four hundred and fifty people?

6. Eight kilometres is about five miles. About how many kilometres is thirty miles?

7. The journey from school to a sports centre took thirty-five minutes each way. The pupils spent two hours at the sports centre. They left school at oh-nine-thirty. At what time did they return?

8. It is possible to seat forty people in a row across the hall. How many rows are needed to seat four hundred and thirty-two people?

9. Pupils spent twenty-five hours in lessons each week. Four hours per week were allocated to science. What percentage of the lesson time per week was spent on the other subjects?

10. A science practical assessment contained two tasks. In the first task all fifteen members of a class scored four marks each. In the second task nine members scored five marks each and the other six members scored three marks each. What was the total number of marks scored by the class?

11. In a test, eighty per cent of the pupils in class A achieved level 4 and above. In class B twenty-two out of twenty-five pupils reached the same standard. What was the difference between the two classes in the percentage of pupils reaching level four and above?

12. Two hundred pupils correctly completed a sponsored spell of fifty words. Each pupil was sponsored at five pence per word. How much money did the pupils raise in total?

13. A pupil scores forty-two marks out of a possible seventy in a class test. What percentage score is this?

14. There are one hundred and twenty pupils in a year group. Each has to take home two notices. Paper costs three pence per copy. How much will the notices cost?

15. What is seven and a half per cent as a decimal?

16. In a class of thirty-five pupils, four out of seven are boys. How many girls are there in the class?

17. In a school there are five classes of twenty-five pupils and five classes of twenty-eight pupils. How many pupils are there in the school?

18. A school has four hours and twenty-five minutes class contact time per day. What is the weekly contact time (assume a five-day week)?

19. In part one of an examination, a pupil scored eighteen marks out of a possible twenty-five marks. In part two he scored sixteen marks out of twenty-five. What was his final score for the examination? Give your answer as a percentage.

20. In a year group of one hundred and twenty pupils, eighty per cent achieved a level 4 or a level 5 in Key Stage 2 English. Sixty pupils achieved a level 5. How many pupils achieved a level 4?

21. A teacher wants to record a film on a three-hour video tape which starts at eleven fifty-five p.m. and ends at one forty-five a.m. the following day. How much time will there be left on the tape?

22. In a year group of one hundred and forty-four pupils fifty-four pupils travel to school on school buses. What proportion of the year group does not travel on school buses? Give your answer as a decimal.

23. A space two point five metres by two point five metres is to be used for a flower bed. What is this area in square metres?

24. In a class of thirty pupils, sixty per cent of the pupils are girls. How many boys are there in the class?

25. A teacher takes pupils in the school minibus forty miles to the regional hockey trials. He estimates travelling at an average speed of twenty-five miles per hour. How many minutes will the journey take?

26. Twenty per cent of the pupils in a school with three hundred and fifteen pupils have free school meals. How many pupils is this?

27. In a practical assessment lasting one hour and twenty minutes a teacher allocated twenty minutes for setting up apparatus. What proportion of the lesson time was available for the actual assessment?

28. A pupil scores fourteen out of a possible twenty-five in a test. What is this as a percentage?

29. Three-fifths of a class of thirty-five pupils are boys. How many are girls?

30. A school's end of key stage mathematics test results for a class of twenty-five pupils showed that nineteen pupils achieved level 5 or above. What percentage was this?

31. What is twelve and one half per cent as a decimal?

32. What is four point zero five six multiplied by one hundred?

33. Two-fifths of pupils starting secondary school in September did not speak English as their first language. What percentage of the pupils did speak English as their first language?

(Continued)

(Continued)

34. A bus journey starts at eight fifty-five. It lasts for forty minutes. At what time does it finish?

35. Twenty per cent of the pupils in Year 10 play hockey. Twenty-five per cent play basketball. The rest play football. There are two hundred pupils in Year Ten. How many play football?

36. For a charity swim twenty-five pupils each swam ten lengths of a twenty-five metre swimming pool. What was the total distance they swam? Give your answer in kilometres.

37. Out of one hundred and forty-four pupils in Year 11, forty-eight do not continue in full-time education. What proportion of Year 11 pupils does continue in full-time education. Give your answer as a fraction in its lowest terms.

38. A teacher travels from school to a training course. After the course is over she returns to school. The distance to the training venue is twenty-four miles and expenses are paid at a rate of forty pence per mile. How much will she receive?

39. A teacher plans to show a twenty-minute video to a group of pupils. The video will be followed by a discussion and then the pupils will take a fifteen-minute test. The lesson will last for fifty minutes. How long can the discussion last?

40. For a practical task a science teacher needs twenty-five millilitres of liquid for each pupil. There are twenty pupils in the class. How many millilitres of liquid are needed?

41. A teacher travelled by train to a GCSE meeting. The return ticket cost twenty-four pounds seventy. She took a taxi ride from the station to the meeting venue which cost five pounds forty pence each way. What was the total cost of the journey?

42. In a test a pupil achieved a mark of forty-nine out of seventy. What is this mark as a percentage?

43. To make a small bookcase in design fifteen pupils each needed two point five metres of wood. The wood costs four pounds per metre. What was the total cost of providing the wood for the pupils?

44. A school trip to a lecture and discussion on one of Shakespeare's plays was planned to leave the school at oh-nine-fifteen. The trip was expected to take one and a half hours each way. The lecture and discussion were advertised as lasting two and a half hours. At what time would the coach be expected to arrive back at school? Give your answer using the twenty-four hour clock.

45. In a school's language GCSE course, pupils had to choose one language. One half chose French, one third chose German and the rest chose Chinese. What fraction of the pupils chose to study Chinese?

3 | Solving written arithmetic problems

Notes

Many of the questions in the skills test will require you to be able to interpret charts, tables and graphs. These are usually straightforward but do make sure that you read the questions carefully and read the tables or graphs carefully so that you will be able to identify the correct information. These questions are so varied that it is difficult to give examples for all of them – practice makes perfect, though.

There are some questions for which you may wish to revise the mathematics.

Fractions and percentages

See the brief notes in Chapter 1 for the essential knowledge. If you have to calculate percentage increases (or decreases), the simplest method is: find the actual difference, divide by the original amount and then multiply by 100 to convert this fraction to a percentage.

Example

Last year 30 pupils gained a level 3 in the National Tests. This year 44 gained a level 3. Calculate the percentage increase.

Actual increase = 14.

Percentage increase = $\frac{14}{30}$ x 100 = 46.667%.

(But note the comment below on rounding.)

Rounding

Clearly this answer, 46.667%, is too accurate. It would be better written as 46.7% (written to one decimal place) or as 47% (to the nearest whole number). You need to be able to round answers to a given number of decimal places or to the nearest whole number (depending on what the question is demanding). The simple rule is that if the first digit that you wish to remove is 5 or more, then you add 1 to the last remaining digit in the answer. If the first digit is less than 5 then the digits are just removed.

Examples: 46.3   = 46 to the nearest whole number
          0.345   = 0.35 to two decimal places
          34.3478 = 34.348 to three decimal places
          34.3478 = 34.35 to two decimal places

$$34.3478 = 34.3 \text{ to one decimal place}$$
$$34.3478 = 34 \text{ to the nearest whole number}$$

Ratio and proportion

These sorts of questions are best illustrated with examples:

Example

(a)   Divide £60 between 3 people in the ratio 1:2:3.

The total number of 'parts' is $1 + 2 + 3 = 6$.

Therefore 1 part = £60 ÷ 6 = £10.

Therefore the money is shared as £10; £20; £30.

(b)   Four times as many children in a class have school dinners as do not. If there are 30 children, how many have school dinners?

The ratio is 4:1 giving $4 + 1 = 5$ parts. Therefore 1 'part' = 30 ÷ 5 = 6. Therefore $4 \times 6 = 24$ children have school dinners.

Don't confuse ratio and proportion. Ratio is 'part to part' while proportion is 'part to whole' and is usually given as a fraction. If the question asked 'What proportion of children have school dinners?' the answer would be $\frac{24}{30} = \frac{4}{5}$.

Notes on measures

You need to know and be able to change between the main metric units of measurement. For example:

Length   1 kilometre = 1000 metres
          1 metre = 100 centimetres or 1000 millimetres
          1 centimetre = 10 millimetres

Mass   1 kilogram = 1000 grams
          1 tonne = 1000 kilograms

Capacity 1 litre = 1000 millilitres = 100 centilitres

Notes on algebra

Generally a formula will be given to you, either in words or letters, and you will need to substitute numbers into that formula and arrive at an answer through what will be essentially an arithmetic rather than algebraic process. Remember the rules that tell you the order in which you should work through calculations.

- **Brackets should be evaluated first.**
- **Then work out the multiplications and divisions.**
- **Finally work out the additions and subtractions.**

Thus: (i) 2 x 3 + 4 = 6 + 4 = 10, but 2 + 3 x 4 = 14 (i.e. 2 + 12) not 20

(ii) $\dfrac{6+4}{2} = \dfrac{10}{2} = 5$

Here do not divide the 6 by 2 which would give 3 + 4 = 7 or the 4 by 2 which would give 6 + 2 = 8.

(iii) 2(3 + 6) = 2 x 9 = 18

Note that some of the questions that follow have several parts. In the actual test each 'part' would be a separate question, for example question 1 could be split into three different questions (one for the mean, one for the mode and one for the median).

Questions

1. There were 30 pupils in a class. Their results in a test are summarised in the table below.

Mark out of 40	Number of pupils achieving mark
19	2
24	8
27	1
29	5
33	2
34	5
36	7

What are the mean, mode and range for these results?

In the test this question could be a 'select and place' question worded as follows: Place the correct values in the summary table below.

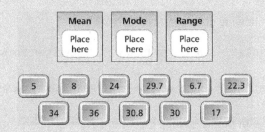

2. A teacher was planning a school trip to Germany. Each pupil was to be allowed €100 spending money. At the time she planned the trip £1 was equivalent to €1.43. When the pupils went to Germany the exchange rate was £1 = €1.38. How much more **English** money did each pupil need to exchange to receive €100?

(Continued)

(Continued)

3. Five times as many pupils in a school obtained level 3 in the Key Stage 2 mathematics test as obtained level 4. If a total of 32 pupils took the test, and just 2 pupils obtained level 5, how many obtained level 3?

4. Teachers in a mathematics department analysed the Key Stage 2 National Test results for mathematics from three feeder schools.

Level	School A Number of pupils	School B Number of pupils	School C Number of pupils	Totals
2	5	3	4	12
3	6	8	8	22
4	16	18	15	49
5	6	3	8	17
Totals	33	32	35	

Which school had the greatest percentage of pupils working at level 4 and above?

5. The national percentage of pupils with SEN (including statements) is about 18%. A school of 250 pupils has 35 children on the SEN register. How many children is this below the national average?

6. A small primary school analysed its end of Key Stage 2 results for mathematics for the period 2011–14. The table shows the number of pupils at each level.

Mathematics	Level 5	Level 4	Level 3	Level 2	N
2014	19	15	7		1
2013	14	18	3		
2012	23	21	4		
2011	21	16	5	5	1

Which of the following statements is correct?

A   The percentage of pupils gaining level 4 or level 5 in 2011 was greater than in 2014.

B   The percentage of pupils who failed to gain a level 5 was greater in 2013 than in 2012.

C   The number of pupils gaining level 5 in 2014 was 5 percentage points higher than in 2013.

7. An end of year assessment for a class of 27 Year 10 pupils was planned to take 6 hours. As part of the assessment each pupil required access to a computer for 25% of the time. The school's ICT suite contained 30 computers and could be booked for a number of 40-minute sessions.

How many computer sessions needed to be booked for the class?

8. A pupil achieved a mark of 58 out of 75 for practical work and 65 out of 125 on the written paper. The practical mark was worth 60% of the final mark and the written paper 40% of the final mark. The minimum mark required for each grade is shown below.

Grade	Minimum mark
A*	80%
A	65%
B	55%
C	45%
D	35%

What was the grade achieved by this pupil?

9. A pupil obtained the following marks in three tests.

In which test did the pupil do best?

Test 1	Test 2	Test 3
$\frac{45}{60}$	$\frac{28}{40}$	$\frac{23}{30}$

10. The bar chart below shows the marks for a Year 7 test.

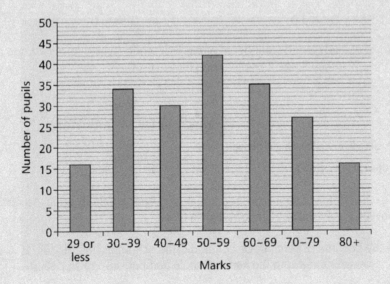

The pass mark for the test was 60 marks. What percentage of pupils passed the test?

(Continued)

(Continued)

11. This table shows the national benchmarks for level 4 and above at Key Stage 2.

Percentile	95th	Upper quartile	60th	40th	Lower quartile	5th
English	97	87	82	73	66	46
Mathematics	98	86	80	72	64	45
Science	100	96	93	87	81	63

Schools' results are placed into categories:

A* within the top 5%;

A   above the upper quartile and below the 95th percentile;

B   above the 60th percentile and below the upper quartile;

C   between the 40th and the 60th percentiles;

D   below the 40th percentile and above the lower quartile;

E   below the lower quartile and above the 5th percentile;

E*   below the 5th percentile.

What grades would be given for the core subjects in a school whose results were:

English   98%

Mathematics   85%

Science   83%

12. A teacher analysed the number of pupils in a school achieving level 4 and above in the end of Key Stage 2 English tests for 2011–14.

	Year			
	2011	2012	2013	2014
Pupils achieving level 4 and above	70	74	82	84
Pupils in year group	94	98	104	110

In each year the school was set a target of 75% of pupils to achieve a level 4 or above in the end of Key Stage 2 English tests.

(a) By how many percentage points did the school exceed its target in 2014? Give your answer to the nearest whole number.

(b) In which year was the target exceeded by the greatest margin?

13. The levels gained in mathematics by the Year 6 pupils in a school in the National Tests are shown below. The results are given for Classes 6A and 6B.

Level	Class 6A	Class 6B
N	1	3
2	2	3
3	11	7
4	11	14
5	5	1
6	0	0

(a) What percentage of the year group gained level 4 or above?

(b) Which class had the greater percentage gaining level 4 or above?

14. Four schools had the following proportion of pupils with SEN.

School	Proportion
P	$\frac{2}{9}$
Q	0.17
R	57 out of 300
S	18%

Which school had the lowest proportion of pupils with SEN?

A School P   B School Q   C School R   D School S

15. This table shows the marks gained by a group of pupils in Year 3 in a mathematics test.

Pupil	Marks	Pupil	Marks
A	23	K	47
B	62	L	38
C	58	M	22
D	35	N	24
E	42	O	81
F	49	P	39
G	76	Q	65
H	80	R	71
I	23	S	73
J	62	T	25

The school will use the results to predict their levels for mathematics at the end of Year 6, and will target those pupils who, it is predicted, will miss level 4 by one level.

(Continued)

(Continued)

This is the conversion chart the school uses to change marks to expected levels.

Mark range	20–24	25–51	52–79	80 and over
Expected level	2	3	4	5

How many pupils will be targeted?

16. A school has analysed the results of its students at GCSE and A level for several years and from these produced a graph which it uses to predict the average A level points score for a given average points score at GCSE.

Use the graph below to predict the points score at A level if the GCSE points score were 6.

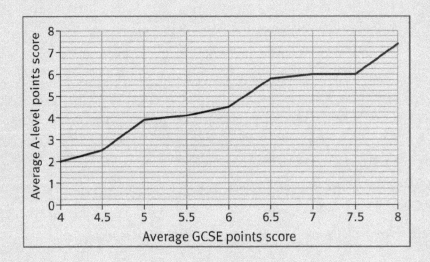

17. A junior school has a weekly lesson time of 23.5 hours. Curriculum analysis gives the following amount of time to the core subjects:

English: 6 hours 30 mins
Mathematics: 5 hours
Science: 1 hour 30 mins

Calculate the percentage of curriculum time given to English. Give your answer to the nearest per cent.

18. A support teacher assessed the reading ages of a group of 10 Year 8 pupils with SEN.

	Actual age		Reading age	
Pupil	Years	Months	Years	Months
A	12	07	10	08
B	12	01	11	09
C	12	03	9	07
D	12	03	13	06
E	12	01	10	02
F	12	11	12	00
G	12	06	8	04
H	12	07	10	00
I	12	06	11	08
J	12	02	10	10

What percentage of the 10 pupils had a reading age of at least 1 year 6 months below the actual age?

19. A teacher analysed pupils' performance at the end of Year 5.

Pupils judged to have achieved level 3 and below were targeted for extra support.

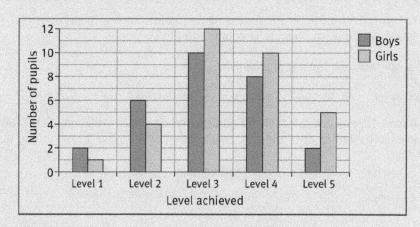

What fraction of the pupils needed extra support?

20. A plastic drinking cup has a capacity of 100ml.

How many cups could be filled from a 1.5 litre carton of juice?

21. A teacher recorded the number of laps of a rectangular field walked by pupils in Years 5 and 6 in a school's annual walk for charity.

(Continued)

(Continued)

Year group	Number of pupils	Number of laps
5	65	8
6	94	10

The rectangular field measured 200 metres by 150 metres.

The teacher calculated the total distance covered.

Which of the following shows the total distance in kilometres?

A 1022   B 1460   C 10220   D 111.3

22. A primary teacher required each pupil to have a piece of card measuring 20cm by 45cm for a lesson. Large sheets of card measured 60cm by 50cm. What was the minimum number of large sheets of card required for a class of 28 pupils?

23. For a GCSE German oral examination 28 pupils had individual oral assessments with a language teacher.

    Each individual assessment took 5 minutes. There was a changeover time of 2 minutes between each assessment.

    A day was set aside for the assessments to take place with sessions that ran from 09:00 to 10:10, 10:45 to 11:55 and 13:15 to 15:00.

    At what time did the last pupil finish?

    A 14:09   B 14:00   C 13:43   D 13:45

24. A teacher produced this table for pupils in Year 5 showing their predicted levels in English, mathematics and science in the end of Key Stage 2 tests in Year 6.

Pupil	English	Mathematics	Science
A	2	3	3
B	5	5	5
C	5	3	5
D	5	3	4
E	4	3	3
F	4	4	4
G	4	3	5
H	4	4	3

What proportion of the pupils were predicted to gain level 4 or above in all three subjects in the tests?

Give your answer as a fraction in its lowest terms.

25. Using the relationship 5 miles = 8km, convert:

    (a) 120 miles into kilometres;

    (b) 50km into miles.

    (Give your answers to the nearest whole number in each case.)

26. A ream of photocopier paper (500 sheets) is approximately 5cm thick. What is the approximate thickness of 1 sheet of paper? Give your answers in millimetres.

27. A teacher organised revision classes for pupils who achieved grades C and D in mock examinations and used the following table to assess the number of pupils who might benefit from attending the classes.

Grade	Boys	Girls	Total
A*	3	5	8
A	4	3	7
B	6	8	14
C	7	4	11
D	4	5	9
E	3	3	6
F	2	2	4
G	1	0	1

    What percentage of the pupils would benefit from attending the classes?

    Give your answer to the nearest whole number.

28. A piece of fabric measuring 32cm by 15cm was required for each pupil in a Year 8 design and technology lesson. What was the minimum length of 120cm wide fabric required for 29 pupils?

29. A school trip is organised from Derby to London – approximately 120 miles. A teacher makes the following assumptions.

    (a) The pupils will need a 30-minute break during the journey.

    (b) The coach will be able to average 40 miles an hour, allowing for roadworks and traffic.

    (c) The coach is due in London at 9 a.m.

    What would be the latest time for the coach to leave Derby?

30. A teacher organised a hike for a group of pupils during a school's activity week. The route was measured on a 1:50 000 scale map and the distances on the map for each stage of the hike were listed on the chart below.

(Continued)

(Continued)

Stage of hike	Distance on map (cm)
1. Start to Stop A	14.3
2. Stop A to Stop B	8.7
3. Stop B to Stop C	9.3

What was the total distance travelled on the hike?

Give your answer to the nearest kilometre.

31. The following table shows the time for 4 children swimming in a relay race.

1st length	John	95.6 seconds
2nd length	Karen	87.3 seconds
3rd length	Julie	91.3 seconds
4th length	Robert	89.4 seconds

What was the total time, in minutes and seconds, that they took?

32. A teacher completed the following expenses claim form after attending a training course.

Travelling From	To	Miles	Expenses
School and return	Training centre to school	238	Place here
Other expenses	Car parking		£7.50
	Evening meal		£10.50
		Total claim	Place here

The mileage rates were:

30p per mile for the first 100 miles

26p per mile for the remainder.

Complete the claim form by placing the correct values in the expenses column.

£40.88   £65.88   £71.38   £73.88   £83.88   £87.00   £89.40

33. A classroom assistant works from 9:00 a.m. until 12 noon for 4 days per week in a primary school and has a 15 minute break from 10:30 until 10:45. She provides learning support for pupils – each pupil receiving a continuous 20 minutes' session. How many pupils can she support each week?

34. The mean height of 20 girls in Year 7 is 1.51m. Another girl who is 1.6m joins the class. Calculate the new mean height.

35. A primary school teacher produces a table showing the differences between the reading age and the actual age for two tests for a group of 16 pupils.

Reading age minus actual age (months)

Test 1	Test 2
−10	−9
−9	−8
−7	−7
−7	−6
−5	−2
−2	0
0	0
0	2
3	4
3	3
3	6
6	7
7	8
9	9
9	10
10	10

(a) Which test had the greatest range in the values of 'reading age – actual age'?

(b) What proportion of pupils made no progress? Give your answer to one decimal place.

36. Equipment for a school is delivered in boxes 15cm deep. The boxes are to be stacked in a cupboard which is 1.24m high. How many layers of boxes will fit into the cupboard?

37. To inform planning a head of science produced a pie chart showing the subject choices made by 150 pupils entering the sixth form. How many more pupils chose to study maths than chose to study chemistry?

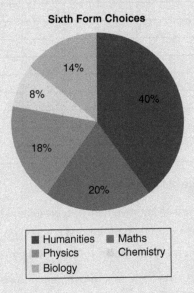

Sixth Form Choices

14%

8%

40%

18%

20%

- Humanities
- Physics
- Biology
- Maths
- Chemistry

(Continued)

(Continued)

38. A teacher planned a school trip from Calais to a study centre. The distance from Calais to the centre is 400km. The coach is expected to travel at an average speed of 50 miles per hour, including time for breaks. The coach is due to leave Calais at 06:20. What time should it arrive at the study centre?

Use the conversion rate of 1km = $\frac{5}{8}$mile.

Give your answer using the 24-hour clock.

39. A newly qualified teacher in his first year of teaching was given a Year 11 class of 20 pupils. As part of his preparation for a parents' evening he studied a table of end-of-term test results for the class.

		Year 10		Year 11	
Name	Test 1	Test 2	Test 3	Test 4	Test 5
A	39	40	41	47	
B	42	44	47	50	
C	42	45	46	50	
D	47	49	48	51	
E	46	48	53	52	
F	50	52	53	57	
G	59	57	58	57	
H	53	55	55	57	
I	55	57	57	61	
J	66	63	65	64	
K	61	60	63	66	
L	56	61	66	68	
M	56	61	66	68	
N	64	66	67	69	
O	51	57	63	69	
P	74	67	69	73	
Q	60	65	71	74	
R	71	73	76	79	
S	75	76	78	81	
T	73	77	82	85	

Class Y11 – End-of-term test marks (%)

(a) Indicate all the true statements.

A   All pupils showed an improvement in achievement between test 1 and test 4.

B   The median percentage mark for test 4 was 65%.

C   The range of percentage marks for test 3 was greater than for test 4.

(b) The teacher expects the trend of improvement shown by pupil O will continue in the same way for test 5.

Write down the correct value for the improvement for pupil O.

Note: In the actual test this question would be worded: 'Select and place the correct value for the improvement for pupil O in the test 5 column in the spreadsheet'.

69	73	75	78

40. Moderators sample the coursework marked by teachers in school. A moderator will select a sample from a school according to the guidelines and rules. One rule that fixes the size of the sample to be selected is:

    Size $(s) = 10 + \dfrac{n}{10}$ where n is the number of candidates in a school.

    What would be the sample size if there were 150 candidates?

41. The SEN co-ordinator for a school explains to the local authority that the proportion of pupils in the school who receive SEN provision is 0.35. The proportion of pupils receiving SEN provision who also have an SEN statement is 0.12.

    What percentage, correct to one decimal place, of pupils in the school has an SEN statement?

    A   0.5%

    B   4.2%

    C   4.7%

    D   2.3%

42. As part of a target-setting programme a teacher compared the marks for 10 pupils in each of 2 tests.

    Pupils' marks out of 120

Pupil	Test 1	Test 2
A	70	66
B	61	68
C	64	63
D	56	41
E	70	78
F	60	59
G	64	77
H	72	80
I	39	44
J	62	57

    Write down the letters for those pupils who scored at least 5 percentage points more in test 2 than test 1.

    (Continued)

(Continued)

Note: In the actual test this question would be expressed as 'Indicate by clicking anywhere on the rows which pupils scored at least 5 percentage points more in test 2 than test 1'.

43. A pupil achieved the following scores in Tests A, B and C.

Test	A	B	C
Actual mark	70	60	7

The pupil's weighted score was calculated using the following formula:

$$\text{Weighted score} = \frac{(A \times 60)}{100} + \frac{B \times 30}{80} + C$$

What was the pupil's weighted score?

Give your answer to the nearest whole number.

44. A teacher used a spreadsheet to calculate pupils' marks in a mock GCSE exam made up of two papers. Paper 1 was worth 25% of the total achieved and Paper 2 was worth 75% of the total achieved.

This table shows the first four entries in the spreadsheet.

	Paper 1 Mark out of 30	(25%) Weighted mark	Paper 2 Mark out of 120	(75%) Weighted mark	Final weighted mark
Pupil A	24	20	80	50	70
Pupil B	20	16.7	68	42.5	59.2
Pupil C	8	6.7	59	36.9	43.6
Pupil D	20	16.7	74	46.3	63

Pupil E scored 18 on Paper 1 and 64 on Paper 2.

What was the final weighted mark for Pupil E?

45. The table below shows the percentage test results for a group of pupils.

Pupil	Test 1	Test 2	Test 3	Test 4	Test 5	Test 6	Test 7	Test 8
A	92	85	87	82	78	26	92	95
B	53	70	72	38	15	27	83	73
C	61	77	69	68	60	30	90	77
D	95	100	93	30	92	30	100	70
E	72	49	47	42	46	82	72	92
F	58	78	38	46	34	58	98	78

Indicate all the true statements.

    A   The greatest range of % marks achieved was in test 2.

    B   Pupil C achieved a mean mark of 66.5%.

    C   The median mark for test 6 was 30.

46. A single mark for a GCSE examination is calculated from three components using the following formula:

Final mark = Component $A \times 0.6$ + Component $B \times 0.3$ + Component $C \times 0.1$

A candidate obtained the following marks.

Component A 64
Component B 36
Component C 40

What was this candidate's final mark? Give your answer to the nearest whole number.

47. A pupil submitted two GCSE coursework tasks, Task A and Task B. Task A carried a weighting of 60% and Task B a weighting of 40%. Each task was marked out of 100.

The pupil scored 80 marks in Task A.

What would be the minimum mark score required by the pupil in Task B to achieve an overall mark across the two tasks of 60%?

48. A reading test consists of 4 parts. The scores are added together to provide a raw score. The table below converts raw scores into an age-standardised reading score.

			Age in years and months					
	6.05	6.06	6.07	6.08	6.09	6.10	6.11	7.00
Raw score			**Age-standardised reading score**					
16	97	97	96	96	96	96	96	96
17	98	98	98	98	97	97	97	97
18	99	99	99	99	99	98	98	98
19	101	100	100	100	100	100	99	99
20	102	102	101	101	101	101	101	101

A pupil whose age is 6 years and 10 months obtained scores of 2, 5, 4 and 7 from the four parts of the test.

What was the pupil's age standardised reading score?

(Continued)

(Continued)

49. A teacher calculated the speed in kilometres per hour of a pupil who completed a 6km cross-country race.

    Use the formula: Distance = speed x time.

    The pupil took 48 minutes.

    What was the pupil's speed in kilometres per hour?

50. A readability test for worksheets, structured examination questions, etc. uses the formula:

$$\text{Reading level} = 5 + \left\{ 20 - \frac{x}{15} \right\}$$

    where x = the average number of monosyllabic words per 150 words of writing.

    Calculate the reading level for a paper where x = 20. Give your answer correct to two decimal places.

51. To help pupils set individual targets a teacher calculated predicted A level points scores using the following formula:

$$\text{Predicted A level points score} = \left(\frac{\text{total GCSE points score}}{\text{number of GCSEs}} \; 3.9 \right) - 17.5$$

    GCSE grades were awarded the following points.

GCSE grade	A*	A	B	C
Points	8	7	6	5

    Calculate the predicted A level points score for a pupil who at GCSE gained 4 passes at grade C, 4 at grade B, 1 at grade A and 1 at grade A*.

52. A candidate's final mark in a GCSE examination is calculated from two components as follows:

    Final mark = mark in component 1 x 0.6 + mark in component 2 x 0.4

    A candidate needs a mark of 80 or more to be awarded a grade A*. If the mark awarded in component 2 was 70, what would be the lowest mark needed in component 1 to gain a grade A*?

53. Over a period of years a school has compared performance at GCSE with performance at Key Stage 3 and established rules for the core subjects which they use to predict GCSE grades. In order to do this they converted GCSE grades to points using the following table.

Grade	A*	A	B	C	D	E	F	G
Points	8	7	6	5	4	3	2	1

For double science the school uses the rule:

GCSE points = Key Stage 3 level − 1

What would be the expected grade for a candidate who gained a level 5 in double science at Key Stage 3?

54. In the annual sports day at a school pupils took part in a running race or in a field event or both. Pupils who took part in both were given an award. In Years 5 and 6 all 72 pupils took part in a running race or in a field event or both.

$\frac{1}{2}$ took part in a running race and $\frac{3}{4}$ took part in a field event. How many pupils were given an award?

55. A school used the ALIS formula relating predicted A level points scores to mean GCSE points scores for A level mathematics pupils. The formula used was:

Predicted A level points score = (mean GCSE points score x 2.24) − 7.35

What was the predicted A level points score for a pupil with a mean GCSE points score of 7.55? Give your answer correct to one decimal place.

56. The head teacher in a primary school collects information about the reading ages of a year group. There are 80 pupils in the year group.

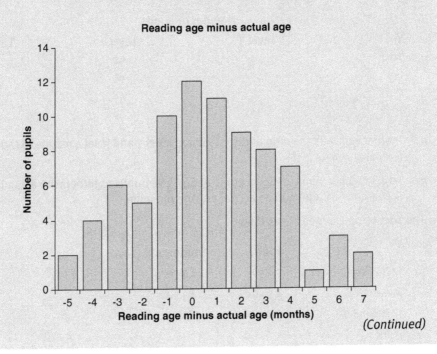

Reading age minus actual age

(Continued)

35

(Continued)

   (a)   What percentage of pupils has a reading age equal to their actual age?

   (b)   Indicate all the true statements.

   A   More pupils have reading ages below their actual age than above.

   B   Six pupils have reading ages of 5 months or more above their actual age.

   C   The range of reading ages in the group is 12 months.

57. An art teacher has £55 in her budget to buy coloured pencils. One supplier is offering a 25% reduction in their catalogue price of coloured pencils. The catalogue price is £20 per box.

   How many boxes of coloured pencils can she buy?

58. There were 27 pupils in a Year 8 history class.

   One pupil was absent when there was a mid-term test. The mean score for the group was 56.

   On returning to school the pupil who had been absent took the test and scored 86.

   What was the revised mean test score?

   Give your answer correct to one decimal place.

59. Teachers in a primary school studied the achievement of pupils over a four-year period. End of Key Stage 2 test results of pupils at the school are given in the table below.

Number of pupils

Year	Level 3	Level 4	Level 5
2011	10	60	18
2012	45	60	25
2013	54	48	26
2014	38	58	24

   In what year was the ratio of the combined level 3 and level 4 results to the level 5 results exactly 4:1?

60. An art teacher plans to take a group of 66 GCSE pupils together with a number of accompanying adults to an art gallery and museum.

The admission charges are as follows.

	Adults	Students
Art gallery	£8.50	£4.50
Museum	£5.50	£3.50
Combined ticket	£12.00	£6.00

One adult is admitted free when accompanying 30 students.

The group visits both the art gallery and the museum.

(a) How much is saved on the total student admission costs by buying combined tickets?

The school requires a ratio of at least 1 adult for every 20 students on educational visits.

(b) What is the cost of the combined tickets for the adults taking into account the free places they will get?

61. A teacher is planning a visit to an activity centre with a group of students. They will use the school minibus.

The round trip is approximately 200 miles. The fuel consumption for the minibus is 32 miles per gallon. The minibus uses diesel fuel which costs £1.34 per litre.

1 gallon = 4.546 litres

What is the estimated fuel cost for the visit? Give your answer to the nearest pound.

62. To inform a staff meeting a teacher prepared a table comparing pupils' results at level 5 and above in maths and science following end of Year 9 tests.

There were 120 boys and 112 girls in Year 9.

Subject		Number of pupils achieving at each level		
		Level 5	Level 6	Level 7
English	Boys	20	48	32
	Girls	10	48	40
Mathematics	Boys	20	56	32
	Girls	12	52	32
Science	Boys	20	56	36
	Girls	16	52	32

(a) In which subject was the percentage of boys achieving level 6 and above greater than the percentage of girls achieving level 6 and above?

(b) What proportion of pupils did not achieve a level 5 or above in English in the tests? Give your answer as a decimal to two decimal places.

4 | Interpreting and using written data

Notes

Some terms, concepts and forms of representation which are used in statistics may be unfamiliar. The following notes are intended to give a brief summary of some of the unfamiliar aspects.

Some of the information received by schools, for example analyses of pupil performance, uses 'cumulative frequencies' or 'cumulative percentages'. One way to illustrate cumulative frequencies is through an example. The table shows the marks gained in a test by the 60 pupils in a year group.

22	13	33	31	51	24	37	83	39	28
31	64	23	35	9	34	42	26	68	38
63	34	44	77	37	15	38	54	34	22
47	25	48	38	53	52	35	45	32	31
37	43	37	49	24	17	48	29	57	33
30	36	42	36	43	38	39	48	39	59

We could complete a tally chart and a frequency table.

Mark, m	Tally	Frequency
9	1	1
10	0	0
11	0	0
12	0	0
13	1	1
and so on		

But 60 results are a lot to analyse and we could group the results together in intervals. A sensible interval in this case would be a band of 10 marks. This is a bit like putting the results into 'bins'.

	13	22	33		
		24	31, 37		
		28	39		
$0 \leq m < 10$	$10 \leq m < 20$	$20 \leq m < 30$	$30 \leq m < 40$	$40 \leq m < 50$	etc.

Note that ≤ means 'less than or equal to' and < means 'less than', so 30 ≤ m < 40 means all the marks between 30 and 40 including 30 but excluding 40.

Here are the marks grouped into a frequency table.

Mark, m	Frequency	Cumulative frequency	
0 ≤ m < 10	1	1	Note how the cumulative frequency is calculated:
10 ≤ m < 20	3	4	← 4 = 1 + 3
20 ≤ m < 30	9	13	← 13 = 1 + 3 + 9, i.e. 4 + 9
30 ≤ m < 40	25	38	← 38 = 1+ 3 + 9 + 25, i.e. 13 + 25
40 ≤ m < 50	11	49	
50 ≤ m < 60	6	55	
60 ≤ m < 70	3	58	
70 ≤ m < 80	1	59	
80 ≤ m < 90	1	60	

The last column 'Cumulative frequency' gives the 'running total' – in this case the number of pupils with less than a certain mark. For example, there are 38 pupils who gained less than 40 marks.

The values for cumulative frequency can be plotted to give a cumulative frequency curve as shown below.

Note that the cumulative frequency values are plotted at the right-hand end of each interval, i.e. at 10, 20, 30 and so on.

You can use a cumulative frequency curve to estimate the median mark: the median for any particular assessment is the score or level which half the relevant pupils exceed and half do not achieve.

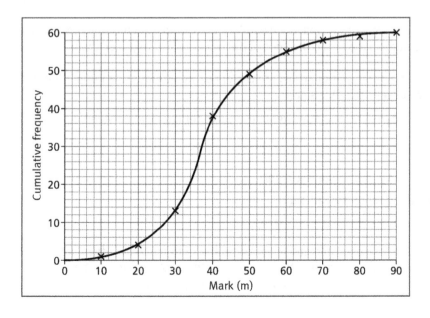

There are 60 pupils, so the median mark will be the 30th mark. (Find 30 on the vertical scale and go across the graph until you reach the curve and read off the value on the horizontal scale.) The median mark is about 37 – check that you agree.

It is also possible to find the quartiles. These are described in the Glossary on page 94.

The lower quartile will be at 25% of 60, that is the 15th value, giving a mark of about 31; the upper quartile is at 75% of 60, thus the 45th value, giving a mark of about 45.

The diagram below should further help to explain these terms. It also helps to introduce the idea of a 'box and whisker' plot.

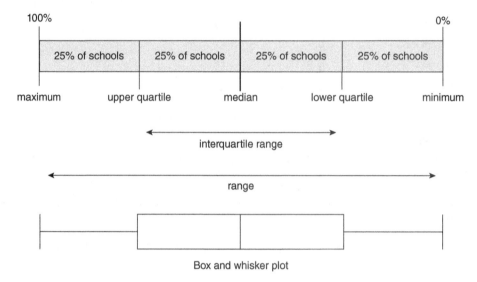

Box and whisker plot

The 'whiskers' indicate the maximum and minimum values, the ends of the 'box' the upper quartile and the lower quartile, and the median is shown by the line drawn across the box.

The 'middle 50%' of the values lie within the box and only the top 25% and the bottom 25% are outside the box. If the ends of the box are close together, then:

- the upper and lower quartiles are close, i.e. the interquartile range (that is the difference between them) is small;
- the slope of the cumulative frequency curve (or line) will be steep.

If the ends of the box are not close, then:

- the interquartile range is greater;
- the data is more 'spread out';
- the slope of the curve is less steep.

You need to interpret 'percentile' correctly: the 95th percentile does not mean the mark that 95% of the pupils scored but that 95% of the pupils gained that mark or lower – it is better perhaps to think that only 5% achieved a higher mark.

The use of percentiles is shown in this table:

Example

Comparing a school's performance with National benchmarks, average NC levels

Percentile	95th	Upper quartile		60th	40th		Lower quartile		5th
English	4.26	4.1	**3.89**	3.89	3.78		3.56		3.36
Mathematics	4.25	3.92		3.85	3.63	**3.63**	3.59		3.24
Science	4.38	4.16		3.91	3.93		3.70	**3.54**	3.49

The figures in bold represent a particular school's average performance.

This table shows, for example, that 5% of pupils nationally gained higher than an average level of 4.26 in the English tests and that 40% of pupils nationally gained an average level of 3.63 or less in mathematics. In other words 60% gained a level higher than 3.63.

The table also shows that the school's performance in English was above average (the 50th percentile) and in line with the 60th percentile, below average in mathematics and well below in science.

Questions

1. A secondary school has compared performance in the Key Stage 2 National Tests with performance at GCSE. The comparison is shown on the graph below.

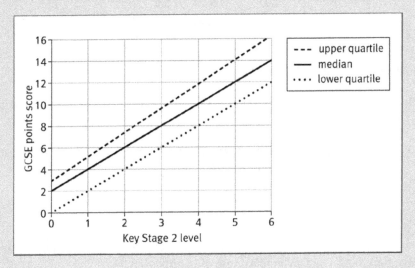

(Continued)

(Continued)

    (a) What is the median GCSE points score of those pupils scoring a 2 at Key Stage 2?

    (b) A pupil had a Key Stage 2 score of 5 and a GCSE points score of 11. Is it true to say that he was likely to be within the bottom 25% of all pupils?

    (c) Is it true that 50% of the pupils who gained level 4 at Key Stage 2 gained GCSE points scores within the range 8 to 12?

2. A teacher produced the following graph to compare performance between an end of Year 9 test and the 2013 GCSE examinations.

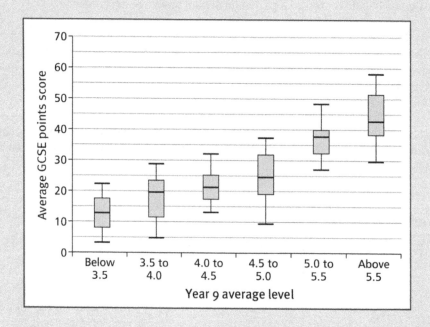

Indicate all the true statements.

A The median GCSE points score for pupils whose average Year 9 level was 5.0–5.5 was 48.

B 50% of pupils whose average Year 9 level was 4.0–4.5 achieved average GCSE points scores of between 17 and 25.

C The range of average GCSE points scores achieved by pupils whose average Year 9 level was above 5.5 was about 28.

3. A German language teacher compared the results of a German oral test and a German written test given to a group of 16 pupils.

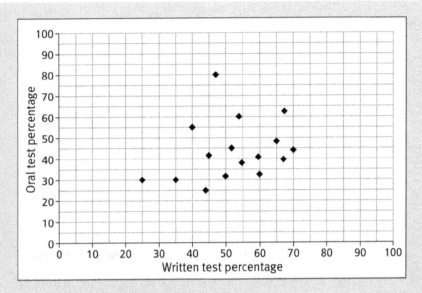

Indicate all the true statements.

A The range of marks for the oral test is greater than for the written test.

B $\frac{1}{4}$ of pupils achieved a higher mark on the oral test than on the written test.

C The two pupils with the lowest marks on the written test also gained the lowest marks on the oral test.

4. A teacher compared the result of an English test taken by all Year 8 pupils.

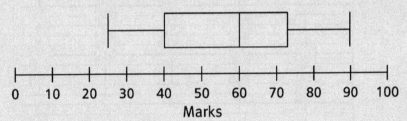

Indicate all the true statements.

A $\frac{1}{4}$ of all pupils scored more than 70 marks.

B $\frac{1}{2}$ of all pupils scored less than 60 marks.

C The range of marks was 65.

5. In 2013 a survey was made of the nightly TV viewing habits of 10-year-old children in town A and town B. The findings are shown in the pie charts below:

(Continued)

(Continued)

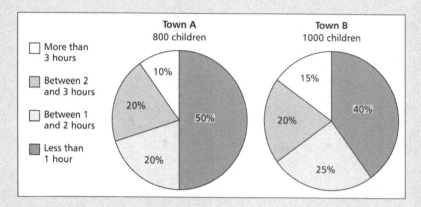

Use these pie charts to identify which of the following statements is true.

A More children in town A watched TV for less than 1 hour than in town B.

B More children in town B watched for between 2 and 3 hours than in town A.

C 100 children watched more than 3 hours in town A.

6. A teacher kept a box and whisker diagram to profile the progress of her class in practice tests. There are 16 pupils in the class.

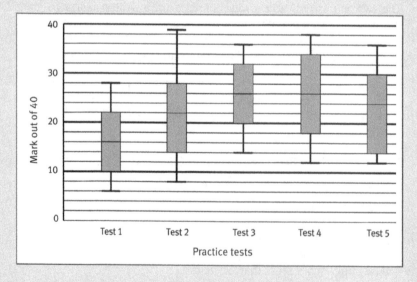

(a) In which test did 12 students achieve 20 or more marks?

(b) Indicate all the true statements.

    A The highest mark was achieved in test 2.

    B The median mark increased with each test.

    C The range of marks in test 3 and test 4 was the same.

7. At the beginning of Year 11 pupils at a school took an internal test which was used to predict GCSE grades in mathematics. From the results the predicted grades were plotted on a cumulative frequency graph.

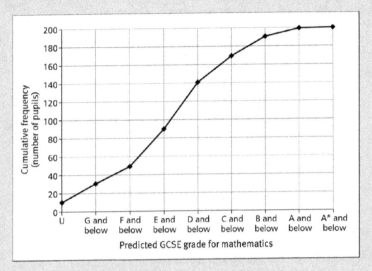

Indicate the true statement.

A 30% of the pupils were predicted to achieve grade C.

B 85% of the pupils were predicted to achieve grade C.

C 15% of the pupils were predicted to achieve grade C.

8. This bar chart shows the amount of pocket money children in Year 7 receive.

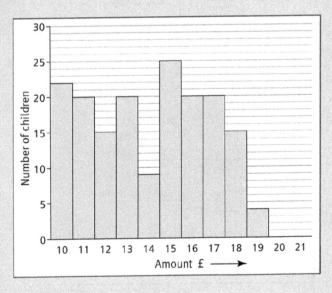

(Continued)

(*Continued*)

(a) How many children were surveyed?

(b) What is the modal amount of pocket money received?

9. A teacher recorded the marks given to five pupils in a series of mental arithmetic tests. Each test was based on 25 questions with 1 mark awarded for each correct answer.

Pupil	Test 1	Test 2	Test 3	Test 4
V	16	16	17	18
W	15	17	16	19
X	14	16	18	18
Y	16	17	18	18
Z	11	13	15	17

Indicate all the true statements.

A The marks for all the pupils increased steadily

B Pupil Z could be expected to gain a mark of 19 in the next test.

C The mean, the median and the mode have the same value for test 4.

10. A Year 7 teacher was given information from feeder primary schools about pupils in the tutor group.

The two box plots below show the reading scores for two feeder schools A and B.

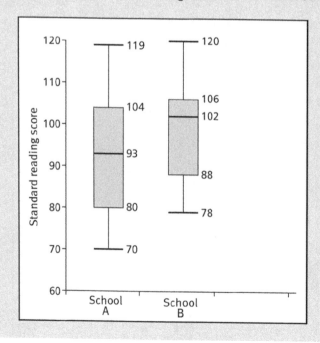

A standard reading score of 100 shows that a pupil's reading score was exactly on the national average for pupils of the same age. Standard scores of more than 100 show above average reading scores and below 100 show below average reading scores for pupils of the same age.

Indicate all the true statements.

A The difference in the median scores for the two feeder schools was 9.

B The interquartile range of the scores for school B was 18.

C The range of scores was 9 less for school B than for school A.

11. Use the box plots and the information from question 10 to indicate the true statements.

A 50% of the pupils in school A had a reading score of 93 or more.

B 25% of pupils in school B scored 88 or less.

C The interquartile range for the two schools was the same.

12. A mathematics teacher prepared a scatter graph to compare the results of pupils' performance in two tests. There were 24 pupils in the class.

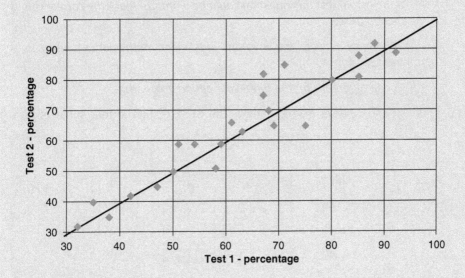

Indicate all the true statements.

A 6 pupils showed no improvement between the two tests.

B A pupil who scored 71 in test 1 showed the greatest improvement in test 2.

C 9 pupils gained a lower percentage in test 2 than in test 1.

(Continued)

(Continued)

13. A teacher compared the results of pupils in a school's end of Key Stage 2 mathematics tests.

	Mean points scored per pupil		
Results in mathematics	2011	2012	2013
Boys	22.5	23.2	24.5
Girls	24.3	24.8	25.6

Difference between boys' and girls' mean mathematics points scores			Mean difference for three-year period 2011–2013
2011	2012	2013	
1.8		1.1	

Write down:

(a) the difference between the boys' and girls' mean mathematics points scores for 2012;

(b) the mean difference for the three-year period 2011–2013.

Note: In the actual test this question could be worded: 'Place the correct values in the shaded boxes for:

- *the difference between the boys' and girls' mean mathematics points scores for 2012; and*

- *the mean difference for the three-year period 2011–2013.*

14. This box and whisker diagram shows the GCSE results in four subjects for a school in 2013.

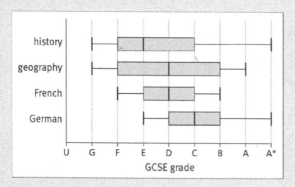

Indicate all the true statements.

A 50% of the pupils who took history gained grades F to C.

B French had the lowest median grade.

C 50% of the pupils who took German gained grades C to A*.

15. The marks of ten students in the two papers of a German examination were plotted on this scatter graph:

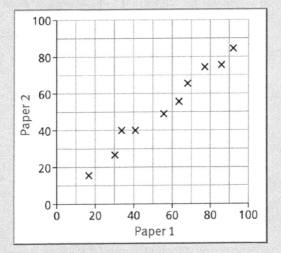

A student scored 53 marks on Paper 1 but missed Paper 2. What would you estimate her mark to be on Paper 2?

16. The straight line shows the mean levels scored in Year 9 assessments for a school plotted against the total GCSE points scores. The points A, B, C, D show the achievement of four pupils.

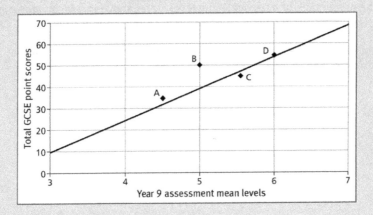

Indicate all the true statements.

A Pupil D achieved as well as might have been predicted at GCSE.

B Pupil C achieved a higher level in the Year 9 assessments than Pupil B but scored fewer points at GCSE than Pupil B.

C At GCSE Pupil B achieved better than might have been predicted but Pupil A achieved less well than might have been predicted.

(Continued)

(Continued)

17. A teacher compared pupil performance in reading in the Key Stage 2 National Tests.

Level achieved	Sex	Year	Percentage of Pupils School	National
3 and above	All	2003	81.8	79.5
3 and above	All	2004	82.3	79.0
3 and above	All	2005	83.4	81.1
3 and above	All	2006	83.6	81.1
3 and above	Boys	2007	78.4	73.9
3 and above	Boys	2008	77.6	74.2
3 and above	Boys	2009	79.0	76.7
3 and above	Boys	2010	79.0	76.4
3 and above	Girls	2011	85.3	84.3
3 and above	Girls	2012	87.1	84.0
3 and above	Girls	2013	88.2	85.7
3 and above	Girls	2014	88.4	85.8

Indicate all the true statements.

A The performance for the school is consistently above the national average.

B Girls outperform boys in the reading tests in the school.

C The percentage of boys achieving level 3 and above increased annually in the school.

18. 20 pupils in a class took Test A at the beginning of a term and Test B at the end of the term.

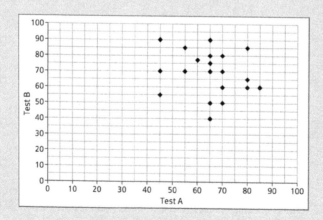

Indicate all the true statements.

A The range of marks was wider for Test A than for Test B.

B The lowest mark in Test A was lower than the lowest mark in Test B.

C 40% of the pupils scored the same mark or lower in Test B than in Test A.

D More pupils scored over 60% in Test A than in Test B.

19. A teacher analysed the reading test standardised scores of a group of pupils.

Pupil	Gender	Age 8+ test standardised score	Age 10+ test standardised score
A	F	100	108
B	M	78	89
C	M	88	92
D	M	110	102
E	F	102	110
F	F	88	84
G	M	119	128
H	F	80	84

Indicate all the true statements.

A All the girls improved their standardised scores between the Age 8+ and the Age 10+ tests.

B The greatest improvement between the Age 8+ and the Age 10+ tests was achieved by a boy.

C $\frac{1}{4}$ of all the pupils had lower standardised scores in the Age 10+ tests than in the Age 8+ tests.

20. The graph shows the predicted achievements of pupils in English at the end of Year 9, based on the results of tests taken at the beginning of Year 9.

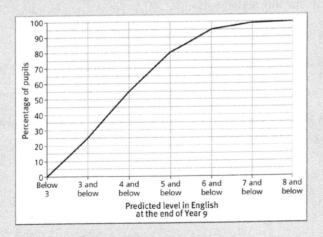

What percentage of pupils was predicted to achieve level 4 and above?

(Continued)

(Continued)

21. Schools in a federation analysed the percentages of pupils gaining 5 A*–C grades in their GCSE examinations over a six-year period. The results are shown in this table.

Percentage of pupils gaining 5 A*–C grades

School	2009	2010	2011	2012	2013	2014
A	47.9	48.6	54.7	54.6	55.8	58.4
B	64.5	64.8	65.0	65.2	65.4	65.6
C	66.1	65.3	64.3	63.7	63.5	63.0
D	49.7	54.7	57.0	63.6	63.7	63.8
E	58.3	59.1	58.5	59.3	58.7	59.5

Which schools improved each year over the six-year period?

22. A research project compared the performance of Year 9 pupils taught mathematics, science and English in mixed classes or in single-sex classes.

This table shows the results.

Median level achieved

Subject	Boys only classes	Girls only classes	Mixed classes
English	7	8	8
Mathematics	7	8	7
Science	7	7	6

Indicate all the true statements.

A The single-sex groups produced better results in science.

B The mixed classes produced better results in English.

C In mathematics girls achieved higher scores than in mixed classes.

23. At a staff meeting teachers were shown a table showing the proportion of pupils achieving level 6 and above in the end of Year 9 tests.

Proportion of pupils achieving level 6 and above in:	Year			
	2011 (%)	2012 (%)	2013 (%)	2014 (%)
English	75.8	76.3	75.8	76.5
Mathematics	69.6	70.2	70.8	71.4
Science	59.0	61.2	62.8	64.0

Indicate all the true statements.

A The greatest year-on-year improvement was for science between 2011 and 2012.

B All subjects achieved a year-on-year improvement over the four-year period.

C The smallest improvement over the four-year period was for English.

24. For a department meeting a head of mathematics produced a box and whisker graph comparing the performance in the end of year tests of four classes in Year 7.

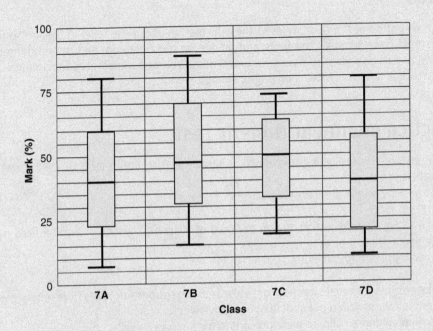

Indicate all the true statements.

A The lowest mark was scored by a pupil in class 7D.

B The median mark in class 7C was 10 marks higher than the median mark in class 7A.

C In class 7B one quarter of the pupils achieved a mark of 70% or more.

5 | Practice mental arithmetic and on-screen tests

Notes

Before you attempt the tests, re-read the information about the tests in the introduction to this book (see page 5), the hints and advice on pages oo–oo, and the opening page of Chapter 2. If you want to time your work, allow yourself 48 minutes to complete both tests. You will find the answers on pages 89–92.

Practice mental arithmetic test

1. Three quarters of a year group of two hundred and forty pupils took part in a sponsored walk for charity.
   How many pupils did not take part?

2. In a GCSE examination forty-five per cent of a school's entry of two hundred pupils gained a grade C or better.
   How many pupils was this?

3. The attendance rate in a school of twelve hundred pupils improves from ninety-five per cent to ninety-seven per cent in consecutive weeks.
   How many more children were present in the second week?

4. Eight kilometres is about five miles.
   On an activity holiday pupils will cycle between two hostels forty kilometres apart. About how many miles is this?

5. Pupils spent twenty-five hours in lessons each week. Four hours a week were allocated to mathematics.
   What percentage of lesson time per week was spent on other subjects?

6. As part of a practical science workshop some teachers will watch a demonstration lesson of 70 minutes which will be followed by a discussion for 30 minutes. If the demonstration started at oh-nine-thirty, what time will the workshop end?

7. A teacher travels from school to a training course. After the course is over she returns to school. The distance to the training venue is twenty-four miles and expenses are paid at a rate of forty pence per mile. How much will she receive?

8. Pupils spent twenty-four hours in lessons each week. Six hours per week were spent on design and technology and art lessons. What percentage of the week is this?

9. A school's end of Key Stage two mathematics test results for a class of thirty pupils showed that twenty-five pupils achieved level four and two achieved level 5. What percentage of pupils achieved level 3 or below?

10. A school minibus travels two hundred miles. Fuel costs twenty-one pence per mile. What was the cost of the journey?

11. A teacher completed a claim form for the number of miles travelled to and from five training sessions. The journey one way was fourteen and a half miles. What was the total number of miles claimed?

12. Two thirds of a class of 27 pupils are judged to be on target for a grade C result in their GCSE mathematics examination. How many pupils are judged to get a grade D result or worse?

Practice on-screen test

1. In preparation for target setting a teacher at a comprehensive school produced a scatter graph showing comparative GCSE results for 2012 and 2013 for 10 schools, labelled A to J, in the local authority.

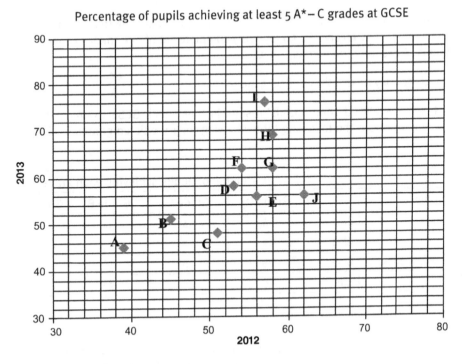

Percentage of pupils achieving at least 5 A*– C grades at GCSE

Write down the letters of the two schools whose percentage of pupils achieving at least 5 A*–C grades at GCSE decreased by more than 2% between 2012 and 2013.

2. A careers teacher produced the following pie charts showing the other subjects taken by sixth form students who also chose to study A level mathematics.

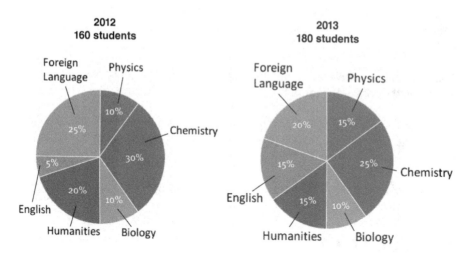

2012
160 students

2013
180 students

Indicate all the true statements.

A More pupils chose a foreign language in 2012 than in 2013.
B More pupils chose chemistry in 2012 than in 2013.
C 10 more pupils chose English in 2012 than in 2013.

3. Pupils in a primary school raise money for charity by collecting tokens from packets of cereal bars. They receive £2.50 for every complete set of 250 tokens collected, with a bonus of £10 for 2000 tokens collected.

How much do they raise if they collect 5140 tokens?

4. A teacher analysed some pupils' results in their mock GCSE examinations in Year 11. She produced the following table showing their predicted grades for English and mathematics.

Subject		Number of pupils achieving each grade			
		Grade D	Grade C	Grade B	Grades A/A*
English	Boys	14	34	32	10
	Girls	13	37	35	15
Mathematics	Boys	28	30	16	9
	Girls	10	45	23	20

Indicate all the true statements.

A The percentage of boys predicted to gain a grade C in their GCSE mathematics examination is greater than the percentage of boys predicted to gain a grade C in their English examination.
B A higher percentage of girls than boys are predicted to gain a grade C or grade B in mathematics.

C The percentage of boys predicted to gain a grade D in mathematics is double the percentage of boys predicted to gain a grade D in English.

5. A local authority gave a primary school a target of 75% of pupils to achieve level 4 and above in end of Key Stage 2 tests in mathematics.

The proportion of pupils actually achieving each level in end of Key Stage 2 mathematics tests is given in the table below.

Level	2	3	4	5
Proportion	0.1	0.1	0.6	0.2

By how many percentage points did the school exceed its target?

6. A teacher produced the following chart to show performance of Year 11 pupils in GCSE mathematics in 2013.

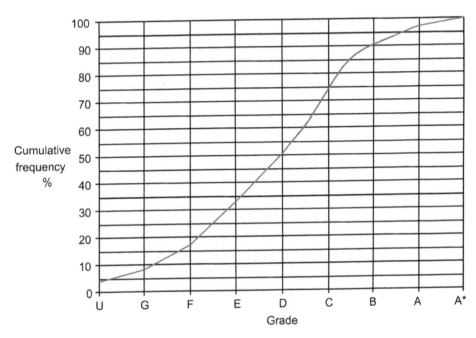

There were 240 pupils in the year group.

What was the number of pupils who achieved a grade B and above in mathematics?

A 10
B 60
C 25

7. The performance in a writing task of pupils in different year groups was determined as part of a research project.

A teacher produced the following diagram to show the levels children reached in writing in the different year groups.

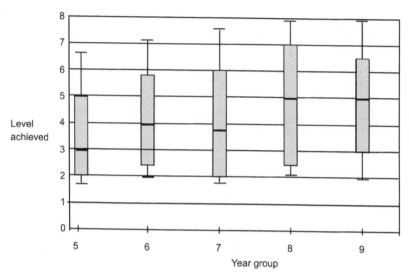

Indicate all the true statements.

A The median writing level decreased between Year 8 and Year 9.
B In Year 9, 50% of pupils achieved a writing level of 5 or more.
C In Year 7, 25% of pupils achieved a writing level of 2 or less.

8. The scatter graph below shows the end of year test results in mathematics and science for a group of Year 7 pupils.

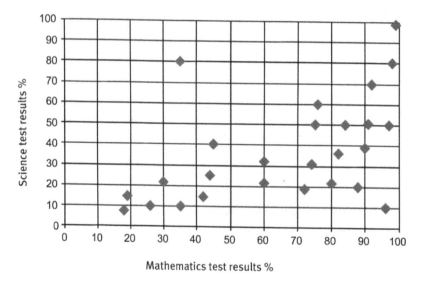

How many pupils achieved more than 60% in at least one of the tests?

9. A head of sixth form uses the following formula to predict A level achievement in points:

$$\text{Predicted A level performance} = \frac{20 \times \text{total GCSE points score}}{\text{number of GCSEs taken}} - 90$$

Student	Total GCSE points score	Number of GCSEs taken	Predicted A level points score, rounded to the nearest whole number
A	28	5	
B	56	8	50
C	45	7	39

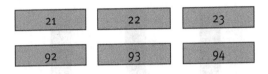

What would be the predicted points score for Student A?

Write (Select and Place) the correct predicted A level performance for Student A in the table.

10. For a trip to Germany pupils have a spending money allowance of £150.

A pupil returns with 30 euros. How much of his allowance did he spend?

Use the fact that £1 is equivalent to 1.2 euros.

11. In a GCSE examination the grade boundaries for each of the three higher tier papers are shown below.

Paper	A*	A	B	C	D	E
Paper 1	90	80	70	60	50	45
Paper 2	90	80	70	60	50	45
Paper 3	180	160	140	120	100	90

A pupil's mark for each paper will be added together to give the total final mark.

The following table gives the minimum total mark required for each overall grade.

	A*	A	B	C	D	E
Total uniform mark	360	320	280	240	200	160

A pupil's mark for Paper 1 was 65, his mark for Paper 2 was 75.

What mark does he need to gain on Paper 3 in order to gain a pass at GCSE grade B?

12. A primary school head teacher prepared a chart showing the percentage of pupils who achieved level 4 and above in mathematics in the end of Key Stage 2 tests.

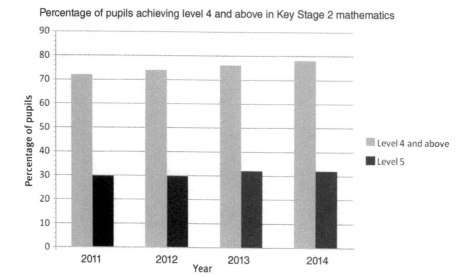

Indicate all the true statements.

   A In each year less than half the pupils achieved below level 5.
   B In 2014, 22% of pupils achieved below level 4.
   C If the trend of achievement continues the percentage of pupils achieving level 4 and above will be 80% in 2016.

13. A sixth form history teacher plans to take a group of 90 students and 6 adults to the site of an archaeological excavation for a guided tour and then to the associated museum.

    The admission charges are as follows.

	Adults	Students
Excavation tour	£5.60	£3.20
Museum	£4.60	£2.80
Combined admission charge	£9.00	£4.50

One adult is admitted free for every complete group of 20 students.

The group visit both the excavation and the museum.

How much is saved if they buy the combined tickets?

14. A teacher prepares a bar chart to compare the percentage of pupils achieving GCSE grades A* to C in mathematics with other GCSE subjects.

    140 pupils sat the GCSE mathematics examination and 90 achieved a GCSE grade A*–C.

Percentage of pupils achieving a GCSE grade A* to C

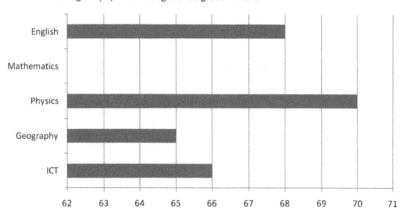

Which one of the following bars ought to be placed on the bar chart above to represent the mathematics results?

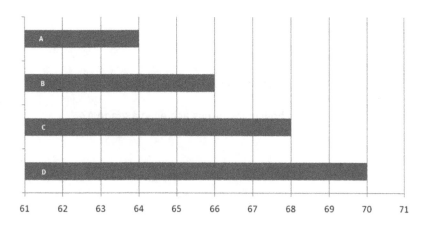

15. This table shows the GCSE grades in design and technology achieved by a school's Year 11 pupils for the period 2011 to 2014.

Grade	A*	A	B	C	D	E	F/G	Total number of students
2011	1	2	2	11	5	6	1	28
2012	6	5	9	13	1	0	0	34
2013	4	7	9	16	4	0	0	40
2014	5	6	8	10	4	2	1	36

Which of the following statements is correct?

A 2012 had the highest percentage of grades A and A*.
B 2011 had the lowest percentage of grade C.
C Less than 1/4 of pupils gained a grade B in any year.

16. A school report includes grades for each pupil's attainment in each subject.

   Grade A is awarded for an average test mark of 72% and above.

Pupil	Mark		Pupil	Mark
A	31		M	7
B	34		N	15
C	12		O	31
D	17		P	23
E	29		Q	26
F	19		R	28
G	24		S	29
H	30		T	33
I	32		U	29
J	28		V	34
K	25		W	30
L	33		X	28

The table above shows the results for an English test for a group of 24 pupils.

If the test was marked out of 36 how many pupils achieved a grade A?

Chapter 1 Key knowledge

1. (a) 4.3   (b) 4.44   (c) 10.09   (d) 5.4   (e) 1.48   (f) 9.19

Key point

Remember to line up the decimal points.

2. (a) 42   (b) 0.35   (c) 2

3. (a) $\dfrac{1}{50}$ (b) $\dfrac{1}{4}$ (c) $\dfrac{17}{20}$ (d) $\dfrac{1}{8}$ (e) $\dfrac{47}{100}$

Key point

Cancel down by dividing both numerator and denominator by the same factor.

4. (a) $\dfrac{3}{8} \times \dfrac{100\%}{1} = 3 \times 12.5\% = 37.5\%$ (b) $\dfrac{13}{25} \times \dfrac{100\%}{1} = 52\%$

    (c) $\dfrac{12}{40} \times \dfrac{100\%}{1} = \dfrac{3}{10} \times \dfrac{100\%}{1} = 30\%$ (d) $\dfrac{36}{60} \times \dfrac{100\%}{1} = \dfrac{6}{10} \times \dfrac{100\%}{1} = 60\%$

Key point

There are different ways of simplifying – which way is best depends on the numbers in the question, but if the denominator is a multiple of 10, it is probably easier to try to cancel down to get 10, as in (c) and (d), unless you are using a calculator in which case change the fraction into a decimal then multiply by 100.

5. (a) $0.25 \times £40 = £10$ (b) $0.75 \times £20 = £15$ (c) $0.12 \times 50 = 6$ (d) $0.2 \times 45 = 9$

Key point

Change each percentage into a decimal.

6. (a) $\frac{2}{3}$ divided by 12, or by 2, then 2 then 3

   (b) $\frac{3}{5}$ divided by 6

   (c) $\frac{2}{5}$ divided by 15, or by 3, then 5

   (d) $\frac{3}{4}$ divided by 25

7. $\frac{39}{60}$

Key point

Change each fraction to a decimal.

---

8. Girls:

   mean   = 50 (to the nearest whole number)
   median = 48
   mode   = 48
   range   = 63 − 45 = 18

For both boys and girls the median, mode and range are the same but the mean for the girls is slightly higher so one could deduce that the girls are slightly better than the boys, but the difference is not significant.

Key point

Make sure you put the values in order before finding the median. See the working out for the boys if you have any difficulties.

Chapter 2 Mental arithmetic

1. 55 minutes

Key point

Count on from 1 hour 20 minutes.

---

2. 28

Key point

70% of 40 = 0.7 × 40 or $\frac{7}{10}$ × 40

---

3.   17

> **Key point**
>
> Note: 100 ÷ 6 = 16.666 therefore 17

4.   75%

> **Key point**
>
> The calculation is 3 x 28 = 84, then (63 ÷ 84) × 100. Note: in a mental arithmetic test the fractions will cancel easily, as here to $\frac{3}{4}$.

5.   9

> **Key point**
>
> Note: 450 ÷ 52 = 8.65, therefore 9

6.   48

> **Key point**
>
> Calculate as 30 ÷ 5 = 6, then 6 x 8 = 48 or 8 ÷ 5 = 1.6 so 30 x 1.6 = 3 x 16 = 48

7.   12:40

> **Key point**
>
> Count on 1 hour 10 minutes + 2 hours.

8.   11

> **Key point**
>
> 10 rows for 400 people, so one more row needed for the remaining 32

9. 84%

> **Key point**
>
> 21 hours remaining $= \dfrac{21}{25} = 84\%$

10. 123

> **Key point**
>
> The calculation is: $15 \times 4 + 9 \times 5 + 6 \times 3 = 60 + 45 + 18 = 123$

11. 8%

> **Key point**
>
> Remember: to convert fractions with denominators of 25 to a percentage, multiply the numerator by 4: $\dfrac{22}{25} = 88\%$, therefore 8% difference.

12. £500

> **Key point**
>
> Simplify quickly by changing into £: $200 \times 50 \times 5p = £2 \times 50 \times 5$

13. 60%

> **Key point**
>
> Common factor is 7, therefore $\dfrac{1}{20}$

14. 720p or £7.20

> **Key point**
>
> Work out as $120 \times 2 \times 3 = 120 \times 6$

15. 0.075

Key point

Think of $7\frac{1}{2}$ % as 7.5% then divide by 100.

16. 15

Key point

Work out as $\frac{3}{7}$ x 35

17. 265

Key point

(5 x 25) + (5 x 28)

18. 22 hours and 5 minutes

Key point

5 x (4hr 25 mins) = (5 x 4hr) + (5 x 25 min) = 20hr + 125mins =20hr + 2hr 5 mins

19. 68%

Key point

18 + 16 = 34 then double

20. 36

Key point

First calculate 80% of 120 which is 0.8 x 120 = 96 (so 96 pupils achieved level 4 or level 5). Then subtract the pupils who achieved level 5, that is 60 pupils, leaving 36.

21. 1 hour 10 minutes

Key point

The calculation is 3hr – 1hr 50 mins

22. 0.625

Key point

The fraction is $\frac{54}{144}$. You now need to simplify this. You might recognise that 18 is a common factor, but if not then divide by 2 giving $\frac{27}{72}$ and then by 9 giving $\frac{3}{8}$. This then is the fraction who travel by bus. Therefore the fraction who don't travel by bus is $\frac{5}{8}$ and you should recognise this as 0.625 Alternatively you could first find the number who don't travel by bus, 144 – 54 = 90. Then express that as a fraction, $\frac{90}{144}$, divide by 16 or keep dividing by 2, and get $\frac{5}{8}$ which is 0.625.

23. 6.25m^2

Key point

The calculation is 2.5 x 2.5. You should know that 25^2 is 625.

24. 12

Key point

Quicker to find 40% or 0.4 x 30 = 12

25. 96

Key point

The calculation is, using the formula: Time = distance ÷ speed, $\frac{40}{25}$ x 60 (the x 60 is to change the answer into minutes) which simplifies to $\frac{8}{5}$ x 60 and then to 8 x 12.

26. 63

Key point

The calculation is 0.2 x 315 = 63.

27. 75%

Key point

The lesson is 80 minutes long. There are 60 minutes left for the assessment and as a fraction this is $\frac{60}{80} = 75\%$.

28. 56%

Key point

With 25 as the denominator you should know that you multiply the numerator by 4.

29. 14

Key point

Find $\frac{1}{5}$ and double to give $\frac{2}{5} \times 35 = 14$

30. 76%

Key point

$\frac{19}{25}$, multiply 19 by 4 to get the %

31. 0.125

Key point

Write it as 12.5 and divide by 100.

32. 405.6

Key point

Simple to multiply by 100 but be careful!

33. 60%

Key point

Either start with the fraction $\frac{2}{5}$ who don't speak English. This is equivalent to 40% so 60% speak English, or work with $\frac{3}{5}$ who do speak English and this is 60%.

34. 9:35

> **Key point**
>
> Treat 40 minutes as 30 minutes + 10 minutes, i.e. 8:55 $\longrightarrow$ 9:25 $\longrightarrow$ 9:35

35. 110

> **Key point**
>
> 20% + 25% = 45% so 55% play football

36. 6.25

> **Key point**
>
> The calculation is 25 x 10 x 25 = 6250 metres, then divide by 1000 to change into kilometres giving 6.25.

37. $\dfrac{2}{3}$

> **Key point**
>
> Either find the number who do stay in full-time education. This is 144 − 48 = 96. Then express this as a fraction and simplify it: $\dfrac{96}{144} = \dfrac{8}{12} = \dfrac{2}{3}$. Or express those who do not stay in full-time education as a fraction and subtract. Thus $\dfrac{48}{144} = \dfrac{1}{3}$ so $\dfrac{2}{3}$ stay.

38. £19.20

> **Key point**
>
> The calculation is 2 x 24 x 0.4

39. 15 minutes

> **Key point**
>
> 20 + 15 = 35 minutes

40. 500

> **Key point**
>
> The calculation is 20 x 25 = 500

41. £35.50

> **Key point**
>
> The calculation is £24.70 + 2 x £5.40

42. 70%

> **Key point**
>
> The calculation is $\frac{49}{70} = \frac{7}{10}$

43. £150

> **Key point**
>
> The calculation is 15 x 2.5 x 4

44. 14:45

> **Key point**
>
> The calculation is start at 09:15, add 3 hours for travelling time and then add 2 hours 30 minutes for the lecture and discussion time.

45. $\frac{1}{6}$

> **Key point**
>
> You need to add $\frac{1}{2}$ and $\frac{1}{3}$. $\frac{1}{2} + \frac{1}{3} = \frac{3}{6} + \frac{2}{6} = \frac{5}{6}$ so $\frac{1}{6}$ study Chinese.

Chapter 3 Solving written arithmetic problems

1. Mean = 29.7; mode = 24; range = 17

Key point

$$\text{Mean} = \frac{19\times2 + 24\times8 + 27\times1 + 29\times5 + 33\times2 + 34\times5 + 36\times7}{30} = \frac{890}{30} = 29.7$$

Mode = most frequent mark, not the number of times it occurs.

2. £2.53

Key point

100 euros = £$\frac{100}{1.43}$ = £69.93 and 100 euros = £$\frac{100}{1.38}$ = £72.46

3. 25 gained level 3

Key point

If 2 gained level 5 then 30 gained either level 3 or level 4. The ratio of level 3 numbers to level 4 numbers is 5 to 1. Divide 30 by (5 + 1), i.e. into 6 equal groups so each group has 5 pupils so 25 pupils gained level 3 and 5 gained level 4.

4. School A

Key point

Percentages are: school A = 66.7%; school B = 65.6%; school C = 65.7%

5. 10 below

Key point

Find 18% of 250 = 0.18 x 250 = 45, so 10 below

6. B and C are correct.

Key point

Looking at actual pupil numbers can be misleading since the totals vary each year. So, in 2011, for statement A. the fraction is $\frac{37}{48}$ and in 2014 it is $\frac{34}{42}$, but the percentages are 77% and 81% respectively.

7. 3

> **Key point**
>
> 25% of 6 hours is 1 hour 30 minutes so 2 sessions (80 minutes) is too short.

8. A

> **Key point**
>
> The calculation is $(\frac{58}{75} \times 0.6) + (\frac{65}{125} \times 0.4) = 0.464 + 0.208 = 0.672$, i.e. 67.2%

9. Test 3

> **Key point**
>
> Convert to percentages.

10. 39%

> **Key point**
>
> Total number of pupils = 16 + 34 + 30 + 42 + 35 + 27 + 16 = 200
> Pupils with 60 marks or more = 35 + 27 + 16 = 78

11. English A*   Mathematics B   Science D

> **Key point**
>
> You need to read both question and table carefully.

12. (a) 1%   (b) 2013

> **Key point**
>
> (a) in 2014 $\frac{84}{110}$ = 76% (b) you will have to work out and compare the percentages for the years 2011–14 – you have already worked out the value for 2014.

13. (a) 53.4% (b) class 6B

> **Key point**
>
> Easy to make mistakes by confusing 'year group' and 'class'.
> Total for each class: class A = 30 pupils, class B = 28 pupils
> Total for year = 58 pupils
>
> (a) Total pupils gaining level 4 or better = 11 + 5 + 14 + 1 = 31
>   As a percentage = $\frac{31}{58}$ × 100 = 53.4%
>
> (b) In class A the percentage = $\frac{16}{30}$ × 100 = 53.3%
>
>   in class B the percentage = $\frac{15}{28}$ × 100 = 53.6%, therefore answer is class 6B

14. School Q

> **Key point**
>
> Change each figure into decimals:
> $\frac{2}{9}$ = 0.222   57 out of 300 = 0.19   18% = 0.18

15. 7

> **Key point**
>
> Look at table 2. To miss level 4 by 1 level thus gaining level 3 means you need to identify pupils scoring marks between 25 and 51.

16. 4.5

> **Key point**
>
> Use a ruler to help – find 6 on the horizontal axis and read off the corresponding value on the vertical axis.

17. 28%

> **Key point**
>
> Because the times both involve half hours, it is simply working out $\frac{6.5}{23.5}$ × 100 = 27.66% = 28% to the nearest per cent.

18. 50%

> **Key point**
>
> Subtract, remembering 12 months in a year. Pupils A, C, E, G, H fit the criterion.

19. $\dfrac{35}{60} = \dfrac{7}{12}$

> **Key point**
>
> Count pupil numbers carefully – jot down totals.

20. 15

> **Key point**
>
> $1500 \div 100 = 15$

21. A

> **Key point**
>
> Number of 'pupil laps' = $(65 \times 8 + 94 \times 10) = 1460$
>
> Total distance = $1460 \times 700 = 1022\,000$ metres = $1\,022$km

22. 10

> **Key point**
>
> Use a sketch – 3 small sheets per width of large sheet.

23. A 14:09

> **Key point**
>
> Remember the last pupil doesn't need 2 minutes' changeover time.

24. $\frac{1}{4}$

> ### Key point
>
> The question says 'level 4 or above'. Remember to simplify the fraction.

25. (a) 192km   (b) 31 miles (actually 31.25)

> ### Key point
>
> The calculations are: (a) 120 x $\frac{8}{5}$ (b) 50 x $\frac{5}{8}$

26. 0.1mm

> ### Key point
>
> Take care with the units – work in millimetres, i.e. 50 ÷ 500.

27. 33%

> ### Key point
>
> The fraction is $\frac{20}{60}$ so as a percentage this is 33.3333%, i.e. 33% to the nearest whole number.

28. 128cm

> ### Key point
>
> You can fit 8 lots of 15cm across the 120cm width.

29. 5:30 a.m.

> ### Key point
>
> Remember time = distance ÷ speed. The travel time = 120 ÷ 40 = 3 hours. Add 0.5 hour, therefore total time = 3.5 hours.

30. 16km

> **Key point**
>
> Total map distance = 32.3cm = 32.3 x 50 000cm on the ground = 16.15km

31. 363.6 seconds = 6 minutes 3.6 seconds

> **Key point**
>
> Add up the time in seconds and decimals of seconds giving 363.6 seconds then convert.

32. £65.88; £83.88

> **Key point**
>
> Remember to work in £ on the mileage rate.

33. 28 pupils

> **Key point**
>
> From 9:00 to 10:30 is 90 minutes ⟶ she can see 4 pupils.
> From 10:45 to 12:00 is 75 minutes ⟶ she can see 3 pupils.
> Total for the day = 7 pupils, total over 4 days = 28 pupils.
> If the calculations were done using the total figures:
>   her working week = 4 x 3 hours less 4 x 15 minutes = 11 hours
>   11 hours = 660 minutes ÷ 20, giving 33 pupils
> This would be incorrect because it ignores the 'structure' of the school morning.

34. 1.514m

> **Key point**
>
> The total height for the 20 girls = 20 x 1.51 = 30.2m
> The new total height = 30.2 + 1.6 = 31.8 m but this is for 21 girls
> The new mean height = 31.8 ÷ 21= 1.514m

35. (a) Test 1   (b) 0.3

> ### *Key point*
>
> (a) The range for test 1 is −10 to 10 which is 20.
>
>   The range for test 2 is −9 to 10 which is 19.
>
>   So test 1.
>
> (b) 5 pupils made no progress so as a fraction this is $\frac{5}{16}$ which equals 0.3125. This rounds to 0.3.

36. 8 layers

> ### *Key point*
>
> The calculation, working in centimetres, is $124 \div 15 = 8.266$, so round down.

37. 18

> ### *Key point*
>
> There are two ways of solving this: The first way would be to (a) find the number studying maths. This is 20% of 150 = 30. (b) Find the number studying chemistry – 8% of 150 = 12, and then find the difference: 30 – 12 = 18.
>
> The second way would be to find the difference in the percentages: 20% – 8% = 12%. Then find 12% of 150 = 18.

38. 11:20

> ### *Key point*
>
> 400km = 250 miles

39. (a) B and C are true.

     (b) 75

> ### *Key point*
>
> The test scores for test 4 are in order so the median is midway between the 10th and 11th pupils' scores. The range is the difference between the highest and lowest scores. In (b) the scores increase by 6 each time.

40. 25

> **Key point**
>
> Sample size = 10 + 150 ÷ 10 = 25

41. B is correct.

> **Key point**
>
> 35% (0.35) receive SEN provision. Of these 12% (0.12) have a statement, so the calculation is 0.12 x 0.35 = 0.042, i.e. 4.2%.

42. B, E, G, H

> **Key point**
>
> Find 5% of 120 = 6 so look for marks in test 2 that are 6 marks higher than in test 1.

43. 72

> **Key point**
>
> Remember to work out brackets first and to round up.

44. 55

> **Key point**
>
> You can check the method by working through the data for Pupil A.
>
> The calculation for Pupil E is $\frac{18}{30} \times 0.25 + \frac{64}{120} \times 0.75 = 0.15 + 0.4 = 0.55 = 55\%$

45. B and C are true.

> **Key point**
>
> Greatest range is test 5 (92 − 15 = 77)

46. 53

> ### Key point
>
> The calculation is $64 \times 0.6 + 36 \times 0.3 + 40 \times 0.1 = 53.2$, i.e. 53

47. 30

> ### Key point
>
> The calculation is $80 \times 0.6 + M \times 0.4 = 60$ so $M \times 0.4 = 60 - 48 = 12$ Therefore $M = \dfrac{12}{0.4} = 30$

48. 98

> ### Key point
>
> Total of the scores is $2 + 5 + 4 + 7 = 18$. Read across the table along the row with 18 and the score in the column headed 6.10 is 98.

49. 7.5km/h

> ### Key point
>
> Speed = distance ÷ time = $6 \div 0.8$ (NB work in hours, 48 mins = $\dfrac{4}{5}$hr = 0.8 hr)

50. 23.67

> ### Key point
>
> You must work out $20 \div 15$ first, not 25×20 then divide by 15.
>
> Therefore reading level = $5 + (20 - 1.33) = 5 + 18.67 = 23.67$

51. 5.51

> ### Key point
>
> The total points are given by $(4 \times 5) + (4 \times 6) + (1 \times 7) + (1 \times 8) = 59$
>
> The calculation is then $(\dfrac{59}{10} \times 3.9) - 17.5 = 5.51$

52. 87

> **Key point**
>
> The calculation is $80 = A \times 0.6 + 70 \times 0.4$
>
> $$80 = A \times 0.6 + 28$$
>
> Therefore $\quad A \times 0.6 = 52$
>
> $$A = 52 \div 0.6 = 86.67, \text{ i.e. } 87$$

53. Grade D

> **Key point**
>
> The calculation is: GCSE points $= 5 - 1 = 4$. Therefore grade $= D$.

54. 18

> **Key point**
>
> $\frac{3}{4} - \frac{1}{2} = \frac{1}{4}$ so $\frac{1}{4}$ receive an award.

55. 9.6

> **Key point**
>
> Work out brackets first.

56. (a) 15%   (b) B and C are true.

> **Key point**
>
> (a)   There are 12 pupils so the percentage is $\frac{12}{80}$ which is 15%.
>
> (b)
>
> A. There are 27 pupils with reading ages below their actual age (i.e. to the left of zero) and there are 41 pupils with reading ages above their actual ages – so not true.
>
> B. $1 + 3 + 2$ pupils have reading ages of 5 months, 6 months and 7 months above their actual age – so true.
>
> C. The range of reading age – actual age is from –5 to +7 – so true.

57. 3 boxes

Key point

The catalogue price of a box is £20. A 25% reduction gives a price of £15. (Remember the calculation is: 20 − 0.25 x 20.) £55 ÷ £15 = 3.67. So she can buy only 3 boxes.

58. 57.1

Key point

Total for 26 pupils = 26 x 56 = 1456. New total = 1456 + 86 = 1542

New mean = 1542 ÷ 27

59. 2014

Key point

Multiplying each level 5 score by 4 should help identify the year.

60. (a) £132   (b) £24

Key point

(a) The cost of separate tickets for 1 student is £4.50 + £3.50 = £8.00. So for 66 students the cost = 66 x £8.00 = £528. The cost of 66 combined tickets is 66 x £6 = £396. The saving is £528 − £396 = £132.

(b) 66 students will require 4 adults (note: 3 adults will only 'cover' 60 students). 2 adults will be free − since 66 is greater than 60. So only 2 adults will have to pay. Cost = 2 x £12.00 = £24.00.

61. £38

Key point

The calculation can be broken down into stages:

- the number of gallons used = $\frac{200}{32}$ = 6.25;
- the number of litres = 6.25 x 4.546 = 28.4125;
- the cost = 28.4125 x £1.34 = £38.07 which rounds to £38.

If you do these sorts of calculations try to avoid rounding any intermediate answers and round when you get the final answer.

62. (a) Science   (b) 0.15

Key point

(a)   Maths:

Number of boys @ levels 6 and 7 = 56 + 32 = 88

Number of girls @ levels 6 and 7 = 52 + 32 = 84

Total number of boys = 120; total number of girls = 112

Therefore % boys $= \dfrac{88}{120} \times 100 = 73\%$

% girls $= \dfrac{84}{112} \times 100 = 75\%$

Science:

Number of boys @ levels 6 and 7 = 56 + 36 = 92

Number of girls @ levels 6 and 7 = 52 + 32 = 84

Total number of boys = 120; total number of girls = 112

Therefore % boys $= \dfrac{92}{120} \times 100 = 77\%$

% girls $= \dfrac{84}{112} \times 100 = 75\%$

Thus in science the percentage of boys achieving level 6 and above was greater than the percentage of girls.

(b)   Total number of boys achieving levels 5, 6 and 7 = 20 + 48 + 32 = 100

Therefore 120 −100 = 20 did not.

Total number of girls achieving levels 5, 6, and 7 = 10 + 48 + 40 = 98

Therefore 112 − 98 = 14 did not.

Total who did not achieve levels 5, 6 and 7 = 34

Total pupils = 120 + 112 = 232

$\dfrac{34}{232} = 0.14655$ so 0.15

Chapter 4 Interpreting and using written data

1.   (a) 6   (b) No   (c) Yes

Key point

(a)   Find 2 on the Key Stage 2 axis and move up the graph until you reach the median line. Read off the value on the GCSE axis.

(b)   Find 11 on the GCSE axis and 5 on the Key Stage 2 axis. The lines through these values intersect in the space between the lower quartile line and the

(Continued)

(*Continued*)

median line so it is not true – remember that 25% of the pupils are below the lower quartile.

(c) Find 4 on the Key Stage 2 axis, 50% lie between 8 (the lower quartile) and 12 (the upper quartile).

2.   B and C are true.

Key point

A.   The median is the line inside the 'box'.

B.   50% is represented by the box.

C.   Range = highest – lowest = 58 – 30 = 28

3.   A and B are true.

Key point

A.   Oral range = 80 – 25 = 55; written range = 70 – 25 = 45.

B.   Imagine a line drawn from (0, 0) to (100, 100). This is the line where scores on both tests were the same. There are 4 points above this line, $\dfrac{4}{16} = \dfrac{1}{4}$

C.   Lowest written marks are 25 and 35, both pupils scoring 30 in the oral, but another pupil scored 25 in the oral.

4.   B and C are true.

Key point

A.   This is false. The upper quartile is at 73, so 1/4 of all the pupils scored more than 73 marks, not 70.

B.   Median is at 60 so true.

C.   Range = 90 – 25 = 65 so true.

5.   B is true.

Key point

It is important to realise that, although the pie charts appear to be the same size, they represent different 'quantities' – 800 children and 1000 children.

Statement A is not true. 50% of 800 = 40% of 1000

(0.5 x 800 = 400 and 0.4 x 1000 = 400)

Statement B is true. 20% of 1000 is more than 20% of 800

(0.2 x 1000 = 200, 0.2 x 800 = 160)

Statement C is not true. 10% of 800 = 80

6. (a) Test 3   (b) Only A is true.

Key point

Remember that each 'part' of a box and whisker plot represents 25%.

7. Only C is true.

Key point

140 pupils get D and below, 170 get C and below so 30 get grade C.

8. (a) 170   (b) £15

Key point

(a) Add up the values given by the tops of each bar:

22 + 20 + 15 + 20 + 9 + 25 + 20 + 20 + 15 + 4

(b) The modal amount is that received by the most children, i.e. £15 received by 25 children.

9. B and C are true.

Key point

A is not true. Pupils V, X and Y have 2 years with the same mark.

B is true – while it is unlikely the indications are that pupil Z's marks go up by 2 each test.

C is true – the mean is 18 – add the marks (=90) divide by 5. The median is 18 – the middle value when the marks are put in order – and the mode is 18.

10. A and B are true.

> **Key point**
>
> A.   Medians are 102 and 93.
> B.   Interquartile range for B = 106 – 88
> C.   School A range = 119 – 70, school B range = 120 – 78

11. A and B are true.

> **Key point**
>
> A.   50% lie above the median line.
> B.   25% lie below the lower quartile.
> C.   IQ range for A = 24 and for B = 18.

12. A and B are true.

> **Key point**
>
> A.   6 pupils on the line of equal scores – so true.
> B.   True – gained 85 and is the greatest distance above the line.
> C.   Not true – 8 pupils below the line.

13. (a) 1.6   (b) 1.5

> **Key point**
>
> (a) Simple subtraction   (b) Simple calculation of the mean

14. A and C are true.

> **Key point**
>
> A.   History 'box' extends from F to C.
> B.   History has a lower median grade.
> C.   German median is at grade C so 50% gained C to A*.

15. About 45–49 marks

Key point

You need to draw in the line of best fit through the points.

16. A and B are true.

Key point

A.   D lies on the line.

B.   C is to the right of but below B.

C.   A is above the line so A also achieved better than might have been predicted.

17. A and B are true.

Key point

A.   Check the school numbers are always greater than the national figures.

B.   Check the girls' numbers are always greater than the boys.

C.   Decreased in 2008.

18. C and D are true.

Key point

A.   Range for A = 85 − 45 = 40, range for B = 90 − 40 = 50

B.   Lowest value for A = 45 and for B = 40

C.   Imagine a line drawn from (0, 0) to (100, 100), 8 pupils on or below the line and $\frac{8}{20}$ = 40%

D.   14 scored over 60% in Test A and 13 scored over 60% in Test B

19. B and C are true.

Key point

A.   Pupil F score decreased.

B.   Pupil B score increased by 11.

C.   Two pupils (D, F) had lower scores.

20. 75%

> ### *Key point*
>
> 25% were predicted to gain level 3 and below so 75% were predicted to gain more than level 3, i.e. level 4 and above.

21. Schools B and D

> ### *Key point*
>
> B and D are the only two schools with values increasing each year.

22. A and C are true.

> ### *Key point*
>
> A. is true – level 7 in science for single-sex classes and 6 for the mixed classes.
>
> B. is not true – the level achieved for the girls only classes were the same as the mixed classes.
>
> C. is true – the girls only classes achieved level 8 compared with level 7 for the mixed and the boys only classes.

23. A and C are true.

> ### *Key point*
>
> A. is true – the actual increase is $61.2 - 59.0 = 2.2$
>
> B. is not true – the English performance decreased in 2013
>
> C. is true – for English the calculation is $76.5 - 75.8 = 0.7$
>
> For mathematics it is $71.4 - 69.6 = 1.8$
>
> For science it is $64.0 - 59.0 = 5.0$

24. B and C are true.

> ### *Key point*
>
> A. is not true – the lowest mark is for class 7A at about 6.
>
> B. is true – the median mark in class 7C is 50, in class 7A it is 40.
>
> C. is true – the 'upper' whisker starts at 70.

Chapter 5 Practice mental arithmetic test answers

Note that units will not have to be entered in the test – the appropriate unit should appear in the answer box.

1. 60

2. 90

3. 24

4. 25 (miles)

5. 84 (%)

6. 11:10

7. (£) 19.20

8. 25 (%)

9. 10 (%)

10. (£) 42

11. 145 (miles)

12. 9

Practice on-screen test answers

1. C and J

> **Key point**
>
> In an actual test this question could be worded as follows: 'Point and click on the letters of the two schools ...' You may find it useful to imagine the line where the percentages are equal for each year, i.e. the line joining (30, 30) and (80, 80). On the screen you could use the edge of a piece of paper for the straight line.

2. A and B are true.

> **Key point**
>
> Note that the pie charts represent different totals.
>
> A. is true – 25% of 160 = 40, 20% of 180 = 36
>
> B. is true – 30% of 160 = 48, 25% of 180 = 45
>
> C. is not true – 5% of 160 = 8, 15% of 180 = 27

3. £70

> **Key point**
>
> Note that you need to work with multiples of 250 and 2000.

4. Only B is true.

> **Key point**
>
> This question refers to percentages. The table gives actual numbers. You will have to calculate the totals for each row.

5. 5%

> **Key point**
>
> The proportion achieving levels 4 and 5 is 0.8. This represents 80%.

6. B

> **Key point**
>
> 75% gained a grade C or below so 25% gained a grade B, A, A*. 25% of 240 = 60

7. B and C are true.

> **Key point**
>
> Look at the notes about box plots if you are unsure how to interpret them.

8. 16

> **Key point**
>
> Imagine a vertical line drawn through the 60% maths result – how many pupils are to the right of this? Imagine a line drawn through the 60% science result. How many pupils are above this line? Be sure, however, not to count pupils twice.

9. 22

> **Key point**
>
> Using the simple on-screen calculator you will need to work out the numerator and jot the answer down, then do the division (here divide by 5) and then subtract 90.

10. £125

> **Key point**
>
> 30 euros = £30 ÷ 1.2 = £25. £150 − £25 = £125

11. 140

> **Key point**
>
> Paper 1 mark was 65, Paper 2 mark was 75. Total = 140. For a grade B pass his total mark must be 280 so he needs to score 140 on Paper 3.

12. Only B is true.

> **Key point**
>
> The trend of achievement suggests that the level 4 figures increase by 2 each year and this would indicate that the 80% figure would be reached in 2015 not 2016.

13. £137.40

> **Key point**
>
> 4 adults will be free. The saving for an adult is £5.60 + £4.60 − £9.00 = £1.20 and for a student is £3.20 + £2.80 − £4.50 = £1.50. Therefore saving = 2 × £1.20 + 90 × £1.50.

14. A

> **Key point**
>
> 90 ÷ 140 = 64.28% so bar A is the best choice.

15. Only A is correct.

> **Key point**
>
> Note that the table quotes actual numbers not percentages so you will need to work these out. For example, in 2012, 11 pupils gained grades A and A*. 11 out of 34 = 32%

16. 16

> **Key point**
>
> First find 72% of 36. This is 25.92, i.e. 26 marks. Next count all those whose mark was 26 or more.

Further reading

You can get further help and guidance with mathematical knowledge from other Learning Matters publications such as:

Mooney, C., Hansen, A., Ferrie, L., Fox, S., and Wrathmell, R. (2012) *Primary Mathematics: Knowledge and Understanding* (6th edition). Exeter: Learning Matters.

Details of publications can be found online at *www.uk.sagepub.co.uk/learningmatters*

Glossary

Accuracy The degree of precision given in the question or required in the answer. For example, a length might be measured to the nearest centimetre. A pupil's reading age is usually given to the nearest month, whilst an average (mean) test result might be rounded to one decimal place.

Bar chart A chart where the number associated with each item is shown either as a horizontal or a vertical bar and where the length of the bar is proportional to the number it represents. The length of the bar is used to show the number of times the item occurs, or the value of the item being measured.

Bar chart showing number of pupils achieving each level

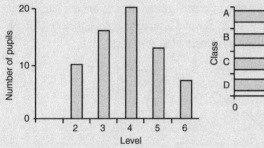

Bar chart arranged horizontally showing mean test scores for four classes

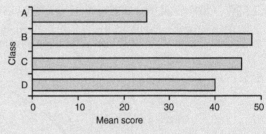

Box and whisker diagram Diagram showing the range and quartile values for a set of data.

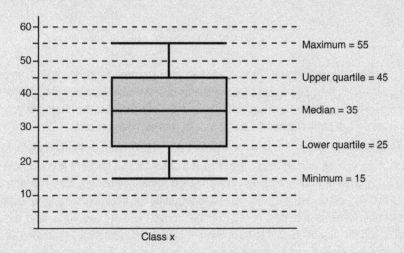

Cohort A group having a common quality or characteristic. For example, 'pupils studying GCSE German this year have achieved higher grades than last year's cohort' (pupils studying GCSE German last year).

Consistent Following the same pattern or style over time with little change. For example, a pupil achieved marks of 84%, 82%, 88% and 85% in a series of mock GCSE tests; her performance was judged to be consistently at the level needed to obtain GCSE grade A*.

Conversion The process of exchanging one set of units for another. Measurement and currency, for example, can be converted from one unit to another, e.g. centimetres to metres, pounds to euros. Conversion of one unit to the other is usually done by using a rule (e.g. 'multiply by $\frac{5}{8}$ to change kilometres into miles'), a formula (e.g. $F = \frac{9}{5} C + 32$, for converting degrees Celsius to degrees Fahrenheit), or a conversion graph.

Correlation The extent to which two quantities are related. For example, there is a positive correlation between two tests, A and B, if a person with a high mark in test A is likely to have a high mark in test B and a person with a low mark in test A is likely to get a low mark in test B. A scatter graph of the two variables may help when considering whether a correlation exists between the two variables.

Cumulative frequency graph A graph in which the frequency of an event is added to the frequency of those that have preceded it. This type of graph is often used to answer a question such as, 'How many pupils are under nine years of age in a local education authority (LA)?' or 'What percentage of pupils gained at least the pass mark of 65 on a test?'.

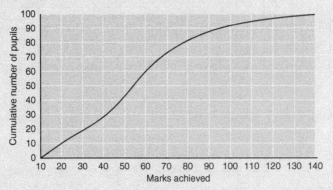

The graph shows the marks pupils achieved. Two pupils scored 10 marks or less, 30 pupils scored 42 marks or less, 60 pupils scored 60 marks or less and 90 pupils scored 95 marks or less. If these were results from a test with a pass mark of 65 marks, then from the graph we can see that 63% of pupils gained 64 marks or less, and so failed the test.

Decimal Numbers based on or counted in a place value system of tens. Normally we talk about decimals when dealing with tenths, hundredths and other decimal fractions less than 1. A decimal point is placed after the units digit in writing a decimal number, eg. 1.25 The number of digits to the right of the decimal point up to and including the final nonzero digit is expressed as the number of decimal places. In the example above there are two digits after the decimal point, and the number is said to have two decimal places, sometimes expressed as 2 dp. Many simple fractions cannot be expressed exactly as a decimal. For example, the fraction $\frac{1}{3}$ as a decimal is 0.3333... which is usually represented as 0.3 recurring. Decimals are usually rounded to a specified degree of accuracy, eg. 0.6778 is 0.68 when rounded to 2 dp. 0.5 is always rounded up, so 0.5 to the nearest whole number is 1.

Distribution The spread of a set of statistical information. For example, the number of absentees on a given day in a school is distributed as follows: Monday – 5, Tuesday –17, Wednesday – 23, Thursday – 12 and Friday – 3. A distribution can also be displayed graphically.

Formula A relationship between numbers or quantities expressed using a rule or an equation. For example, final mark = (0.6 x mark 1) + (0.4 x mark 2).

Fraction Fractions are used to express parts of a whole, eg. $\frac{3}{4}$. The number below the division line, the denominator, records the number of equal parts into which the number above the division line, the numerator, has been divided.

Frequency The number of times an event or quantity occurs.

Greater than A comparison between two quantities. The symbol > is used to represent 'greater than', eg. 7>2, or >5%.

Interquartile range The numerical difference between the upper quartile and the lower quartile. The lower quartile of a set of data has one quarter of the data below it and three-quarters above it. The upper quartile has three quarters of the data below it and one quarter above it. The inter-quartile range represents the middle 50% of the data.

Line graphs A graph on which the plotted points are joined by a line. It is a visual representation of two sets of related data. The line may be straight or curved. It is often used to show a trend, such as how a particular value is changing over time.

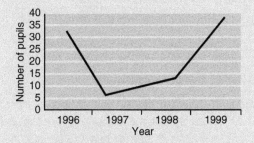

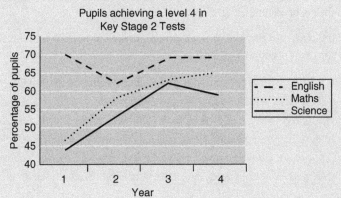

Mean One measure of the 'average' of a set of data. The 'mean' average is usually used when the data involved is fairly evenly spread. For example, the individual costs of four textbooks are £9.95, £8.34, £11.65 and £10.50. The mean cost of a textbook is found by totalling the four amounts, giving £40.44, and then dividing by 4, which gives £10.11. The word average is frequently used in place of the mean, but this can be confusing as both median and mode are also ways of expressing an average.

Median Another measure of the 'average' of a set of data. It is the middle number of a series of numbers or quantities when arranged in order, eg. from smallest to largest. For example, in the following series of number: 2, 4, 5, 7, 8, 15 and 18, the median is 7. When there is an even number of numbers, the median is found by adding the two middle numbers and then halving the total. For example, in the following series of numbers, 12, 15, 23, 30, 31 and 45, the median is $(23 + 30) \div 2 = 26.5$.

Median and quartile lines Quartiles can be found by taking a set of data that has been arranged in increasing order and dividing it into four equal parts. The first quartile is the value of the data at the end of the first quarter. The median quartile is the value of the data at the end of the second quarter. The third quartile is the value of the data at the end of the third quarter.

Quartile lines can be used to show pupils' progression from one key stage to another, when compared with national or local data:

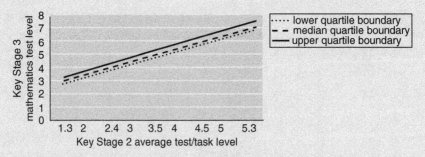

Mode Another measure of the 'average' of a set of data. It is the most frequently occurring result in any group of data. For example, in the following set of exam results: 30%, 34%, 36% 31%, 31%, 30%, 34%, 33%, 31% and 32%, the mode is 31% because this value appears most frequently in the set of results.

Operations The means of combining two numbers or sets of numbers. For example, addition, subtraction, multiplication and division.

Percentage A fraction with a denominator of 100, but written as the numerator followed by '%', e.g. $\frac{30}{100}$ or 30%. A fraction that is not in hundredths can be converted so that the denominator is 100, e.g. $\frac{650}{1000} = \frac{65}{100} = 65\%$. Percentages can be used to compare different fractional quantities. For example, in class A, 10 pupils out of 25 are studying French; in class B, 12 out of 30 pupils are studying French. However, both $\frac{10}{25}$ and $\frac{12}{30}$ are equivalent to $\frac{4}{10}$, or 40%. The same percentage of pupils, therefore, study French in both these classes.

Percentage points The difference between two values, given as percentages. For example, a school has 80% attendance one year and 83% the next year. There has been an increase of 3 percentage points in attendance.

Percentile The values of a set of data that has been arranged in order and divided into 100 equal parts. For example, a year group took a test and the 60th percentile was at a mark of 71. This means that 60% of the cohort scored 71 marks or less. The 25th percentile is the value of the data such that 25% or one quarter of the data is below it and so is the same as the lower quartile. Similarly, the 75th percentile is the same as the upper quartile and the median is the same as the 50th percentile.

Pie chart A pie chart represents the 360° of a circle and is divided into sectors by straight lines from its centre to its circumference. Each sector angle represents a specific proportion of the whole. Pie charts are used to display the relationship of each type or class of data within a whole set of data in a visual form.

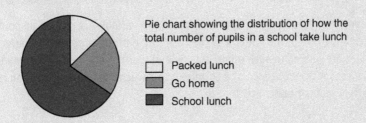

Pie chart showing the distribution of how the total number of pupils in a school take lunch

- ☐ Packed lunch
- ▨ Go home
- ▰ School lunch

Prediction A statement based on analysing statistical information about the likelihood that a particular event will occur. For example, an analysis of a school's examination results shows that the number of pupils achieving A*–C grades in science at a school has increased by 3% per year over the past three years. On the basis of this information the school predicts that the percentage of pupils achieving A*–C grades in science at the school next year will increase by at least 2%.

Proportion A relationship between two values or measures. These two values or measures represent the relationship between some part of a whole and the whole itself. For example, a year group of 100 pupils contains 60 boys and 40 girls, so the proportion of boys in the school is 60 out of 100 or 3 out of 5. This is usually expressed as a fraction, in this case, $\frac{3}{5}$.

Quartile (lower) The value of a set of data at the first quarter, 25%, when all the data has been arranged in ascending order. It is the median value of the lower half of all the values in the data set. For example, the results of a test were: 1, 3, 5, 6, 7, 9, 11, 15, 18, 21, 23 and 25. The median is 10. The values in the lower half are 1, 3, 5, 6, 7 and 9. The lower quartile is 5.5. This means that one quarter of the cohort scored 5.5 or less. The lower quartile is also the 25th percentile.

Quartile (upper) The value of a set of data at the third quarter, 75%, when that data has been arranged in ascending order. It is the median value of the upper half of all the values in the data set. In the lower quartile example, the upper quartile is 19.5, the median value of the upper half of the data set. Three quarters of the marks lie below it. The upper quartile is also the 75th percentile.

Range The difference between the lowest and the highest values in a set of data. For example, for the set of data 12, 15, 23, 30, 31 and 45, the range is the difference between 12 and 45. 12 is subtracted from 45 to give a range of 33.

Ratio A comparison between two numbers or quantities. A ratio is usually expressed in whole numbers. For example, a class consists of 12 boys and 14 girls. The ratio of boys to girls is 12:14. This ratio may be described more simply as 6:7 by dividing both numbers by 2. The ratio of girls to boys is 14:12 or 7:6.

Rounding Expressing a number to a degree of accuracy. This is often done in contexts where absolute accuracy is not required, or not possible. For example, it may be acceptable in a report to give outcomes to the nearest hundred or ten. So the number 674 could be rounded up to 700 to the nearest hundred, or down to 670 to the nearest ten. If a number is half way or more between rounding points, it is conventional to round it up, eg. 55 is rounded up to 60 to the near-est ten and 3.7 is rounded up to 4 to the nearest whole number. If the number is less than half way, it is conventional to round down, eg. 16.43 is rounded down to 16.4 to one decimal place.

Scatter graph A graph on which data relating to two variables is plotted as points, each axis representing one of the variables. The resulting pattern of points indicates how the two variables are related to each other. This type of graph is often used to demonstrate or confirm the presence or absence of a correlation between the two variables, and to judge the strength of that correlation.

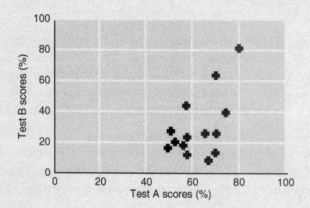

Sector The part or area of a circle which is formed between two radii and the circumference. Each piece of a pie chart is a sector.

Standardised scores Standardised scores are used to enable comparisons on tests between different groups of pupils. Tests are standardised so that the average national standardised scores automatically appear as 100, so it is easy to see whether a pupil is above or below the national average.

Trend The tendency of data to follow a pattern or direction. For example, the trend of the sequence of numbers 4, 7, 11, 13 and 16 is described as 'increasing'.

Value added The relationship between a pupil's previous attainment and their current attain-ment gives a measure of their progress. Comparing this with the progress made by other pupils gives an impression of the value added by a school. Below is a scatter graph showing progress made by a group of pupils between the end of Key Stage 1 and the end of Key Stage 2:

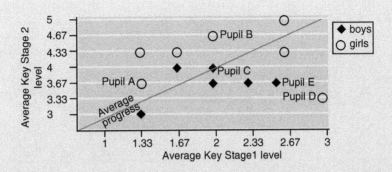

The 'trend line' shows the average performance. Pupils above the line, such as A and B, made better progress than expected; those below the line, such as pupils E and D made less progress than that expected.

How Key Stage 2 relates to Key Stage 1: Median, upper and lower quartile

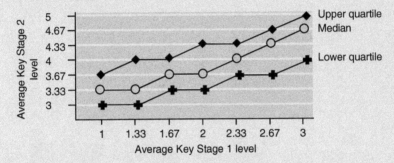

Here the median line shows the national average progress.

Variables The name given to a quantity which can take any one of a given set of values. For example, on a line graph showing distance against time, both distance and time are variables. A variable can also be a symbol which stands for an unknown number, and that can take on different values. For example, the final mark in a test is obtained by a formula using the variables A and B as follows: final mark= (Topic 1 mark x A) + (Topic 2 mark x B).

Weighting A means of attributing relative importance to one or more of a set of results. Each item of data is multiplied by a pre-determined amount to give extra weight to one or more components. For example, marks gained in year 3 of a course may be weighted twice as heavily as those gained in the first two years, in which case those marks would be multiplied by two before finding the total mark for the course.

Whole number A positive integer, eg. 1, 2, 3, 4, 5.

© Teaching Agency

Contents

Preface

I have worked with healthcare professionals for many years teaching language and communication skills. I was approached to write this handbook as the publisher had been made aware of the needs of care workers working with dementia patients. The care home managers had remarked how communicating with dementia patients could be quite difficult for anyone, while in the care system there is a high number of workers with English as a second language. Communication was even more problematic for this group of people.

During my time doing all the background reading I became totally absorbed in the subject. The amount of work and research being done by many, many people and groups is incredible. All over the world people are contributing to the numerous debates about caring for people with dementia.

There are many approaches and many different schools of thought but through them all runs the same thread. Don't look at the dementia – look at the person! All people with dementia are individuals with different needs, different histories and different behaviours. Graham Stokes (2010) talks about looking at the uniqueness of each dementia patient, not their similarities, and goes on to say, 'Can we really say that whatever a person with dementia does, it is because they have dementia?' (p.54). Tom Kitwood, a leading expert in dementia, talks about 'personhood' (how a person is regarded by others) and states that a judge of how successful the dementia care is, is how long the person keeps their personhood (Epp, 2003).

I have had two influences whilst planning and writing the book. I have an MA in Human Rights and Equal Opportunities, so it is not surprising I view the issue from this perspective. Also, as with many people in my age group, the awareness that dementia will affect so many of us is often in my mind. I am filled with horror at the thought of being in a position where, even though I will probably be physically comfortable, well fed and kept clean, I may be living without meaningful communication, without understanding and without human contact at the emotional level. Gemma Jones (1992), cited in Goldsmith (1996), compared life in many care homes to being sent into solitary confinement without a trial!

So there is all this information, all these incredible books, all these passionate people – all almost pleading with carers to rethink their views on people with dementia, to look at them with fresh eyes, to see the person within and to try to respond to their individual needs. It was with this in mind that I worked out what to put in this handbook – how to make the information more accessible. Accessible to all carers with English as a second language working in care homes, hospitals, hospices, home support or any other supporting environment.

Aimed at these carers I have:
- simplified the language
- brought a range of information from many sources into one accessible handbook
- given basic information on dementia
- described good communication skills when working with people with dementia
- supplied language that can be used when talking to people with dementia
- talked about communicating with people in later stages of dementia
- given ideas on how to socially interact by involving the individuals in different activities
- developed vocabulary needed to read or talk about caring for dementia patients
- given carers the opportunity to link the ideas in the book to their own experiences at work by making notes in their 'notebook'
- directed carers to other sources of information.

There are many training courses for carers of people with dementia, but I found only one for carers with English as a second language (run by Stirling County Council). Hopefully this handbook can be used either by the care worker as a self-study aid or alongside any of the available training courses.

I hope readers will use this handbook to help them in their work and also to direct them to further reading on the topic.

I would like to thank my husband, Edgar, a care worker with English as a second language, working with people with dementia – mainly in the later stages of the disease – who shared his thoughts, observations and frustrations with me. Also, my daughter, Charlotte, who worked thoughtfully on the illustrations, Gillian Nineham, Editorial Director at Radcliffe, who patiently led me through the whole process, and all the organisations and individuals who freely and immediately allowed me to use their work and publications.

Rita Salomon

October 2013

About the author

Rita Salomon has been teaching English as a second language, together with communication skills, since 1995. She has worked with a whole range of healthcare professionals from overseas: GPs, consultants, nurses, physiotherapists and dentists. Not a medical professional herself, her work has been to help these professionals to improve their English language and communication skills to aid interaction with their patients/clients. Much of her work was done for the NHS in the UK but some was delivered overseas, preparing GPs in Poland for their OSCE examinations in the UK and a three-year stint in a military hospital in Saudi Arabia.

She first became interested in dementia after reading *Still Alice* by Lisa Genova (2009). This, together with her husband working as a care worker with people in the later stages of dementia, ignited her passion for the subject. Her MA in Human Rights and Equal Opportunities influenced her in viewing the topic from this perspective.

Introduction

Aims of the book

This book is for healthcare workers who are based in a care setting working with elderly people and people with dementia. Their first language is not English but they have to use English to communicate with clients/patients, their families and colleagues.

There has been much news coverage of the dementia 'explosion' with talk of a 'ticking time bomb'. The rise in the number of people with dementia is causing concerns worldwide. As the population ages and life expectancy lengthens then the number of people with dementia will go on increasing.

Look at the statistics from The Alzheimer's Society.
- In 2012 there were 800,000 people with dementia in the UK.
- There will be over a million people with dementia by 2021.
- 60,000 deaths a year are directly attributable to dementia.
- The financial cost of dementia to the UK will be over £23 billion in 2012.
- 80% of people living in care homes have a form of dementia or severe memory problems.

   (www.alzheimers.org.uk/statistics)

The Government's response reflects its concern.
- The government took note of the report from the Alzheimer's Association, *Early Onset Dementia: a national challenge, a future crisis* (2006), calling it the Dementia Challenge.

- The Dementia Friends programme – a national initiative that is being run by the Alzheimer's Society. It is funded by the government and aims to improve people's understanding of dementia and its effects.

- The next phase of the Dementia Challenge measures (announced in November 2012) include

  - £9.6 million for dementia research

  - extra support for GPs on dementia

  - pilot with schools and youth projects

  - £1 million prize fund for ways to increase diagnosis

  - £50 million fund for environments designed for people with dementia

  - commitment to providing information for people diagnosed with dementia.

- In April 2013, the National Institute for Health and Care Excellence (NICE) published their Quality Standard QS30 – '**Quality standard for supporting people to live well with dementia**'. NICE is accountable to its sponsor department, the Department of Health, but operationally is independent of government.

- In May 2013, Health Secretary Jeremy Hunt warned that dementia had replaced cancer as the biggest challenge facing the NHS and all dementia patients were to get a personal carer (*i* newspaper, 13 May 2013).

- Also in May 2013, in the Queen's speech, it was stated that the government had made care for the elderly a priority in its plans for the NHS.

- David Cameron stated that the UK would use its Presidency of the G8 in 2013 to identify and agree a new international approach on dementia research in recognition that the condition is fast becoming the biggest pressure on care systems around the world. A specific G8 dementia summit would be held in London in September 2013, bringing together experts from around the world. The event would look to secure more coordination and collaboration on dementia globally (Department of Health, 2013).

It is plain to see that care for people with dementia is an area of great concern with huge growth forecast in the coming years.

As reflected in the NICE Quality Standard, the emphasis is swinging away from focusing on the symptoms of dementia, focusing instead on helping that person to live well. The carer needs to see beyond the dementia, to see the person within. The medical model of dementia is being replaced by the social model. The person-centred approach is at the heart of care for dementia patients.

With this in mind, the care of these patients is not just about washing, feeding, and so on, but about keeping each individual at the heart of the care plan and ensuring the dignity and 'personhood' of each one. Much of this involves good communication skills.

The care worker in the care home, hospice or hospital is often the one putting these theories into practice. Many of these workers have English as a second language. It is the aim of this handbook to help the carer to understand the basics of dementia, to give an insight into what is involved in good communication to enable them to interact with the person within and to provide the language needed for positive interaction.

Layout of the book

The book is divided into five main parts.

Part 1 Dementia – What's it all about?
Includes general facts and the current thinking about care for dementia patients in the UK.

Part 2 Communicating – How do I get through?
Includes what is involved in good communication and looks briefly at communication in the later stages of dementia.

Part 3 Language – What do I say?
Includes functional language needed to show empathy, concern, reassurance, and so on.

Part 4   Challenging behaviour – How do I react?

Lists the most common behaviours associated with dementia, describes them and suggests how to react to them.

Part 5   Encouraging conversation and activity – What can I do?

Includes how to encourage social conversation and interaction, the usefulness of activities and looks at some available resources.

How to use this book

This book can be used by the individual as a self-study resource. It can also be used on a dementia course as additional support for members with English as a second language (ESL). For those places with a high number of ESL carers it could be a course book for a course specifically for them.

The **Word Check** tables throughout the book are a way of building up vocabulary needed for the work place and also to study the topic further. The reader has the opportunity to translate the words into their own language after looking up the meanings in the Word Check section at the back of the book.

The **English Check** sections give the opportunity to practise the language covered in the different sections. This could be with gap-fill sentences to check meanings of words or in mini dialogues to practise language.

The **Notebook** gives the reader the opportunity to link the ideas in the book to their work practices.

References to Internet sites, articles and books are made throughout to enable further reading and study.

This handbook is seen as just an introduction to the developing and expanding study of working with people with dementia.

Part 1

Dementia –
What's it all about?

Dementia – What's it all about?

What do you think of when you hear the word 'dementia'?

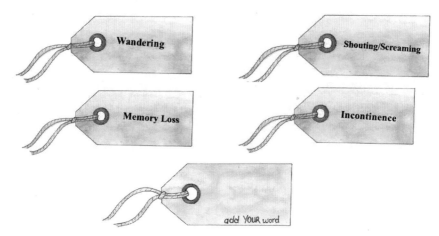

Figure 1.1 Labelling dementia?

What do you think a person with dementia thinks of dementia?

> *What do you see, nurses,*
> *what do you see?*
> *What are you thinking when*
> *you're looking at me?*
> *A crabby old woman, not very wise,*
> *Uncertain of habit, with faraway eyes?*
> *Who dribbles her food and makes no reply*
> *When you say in a loud voice, 'I do wish you'd try!'*
> *Who seems not to notice the things that you do,*
> *And forever is losing a stocking or shoe...*
> *Who, resisting or not, lets you do as you will,*
> *With bathing and feeding, the long day to fill...*
> *Is that what you're thinking? Is that what you see?*
> *Then open your eyes, nurse;*
> *you're not looking at me.*
>
> ('An Old Woman's Poem' – Anonymous. For complete poem see Appendix 1.)

Figure 1.2 The thoughts of a dementia patient

Christine Bryden, a person with dementia, describes how she is deteriorating throughout her disease.

·That high-powered, cool, calm and collected person has become lost and forgotten along the way. Now I am slow, emotionally unpredictable and confused in a maze of words, numbers and endless 'thingys'.

Figure 1.3 What does a person with dementia think? (Bryden, 2012)

Basic information about dementia

Word Check 1

Check	✓	Meaning/translation
symptoms		
agitation		
memory		
functions		
frustrated		
empathise		

What is dementia?

It is important to have a basic understanding of what dementia is as this will help you to understand the behaviour and empathise with the person with dementia.

Dementia is not the name of a single illness but of several symptoms which affect the working of the brain – it affects the functions of the brain. These functions include making decisions and judgements. Memory is affected and most people with dementia forget many things, even the names of their close family. Remembering dates and the names of places they used to know well is also a problem. This forgetfulness causes frustration and agitation, sometimes anger. Many people become depressed as a result.

Not everybody gets dementia as they get older.

What causes dementia?

Word Check 2

Check	✔	*Meaning/translation*
a stroke		
tangles		
risk		
genetic		
spherical		
abnormal		

Dementia is caused by damage to brain cells which can be caused in different ways depending on the form of dementia.

There are several forms of dementia. Symptoms are not identical as different parts of the brain are affected by each form of dementia. The most common are as follows.

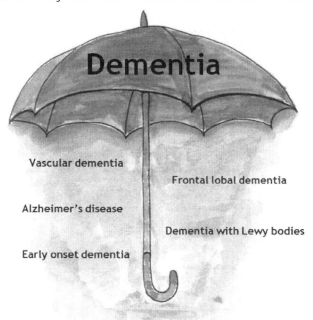

Figure 1.4 Different forms of dementia (Tan, 2010)

Alzheimer's disease. The actual cause of Alzheimer's is not known but 'tangles' can be seen in the brain and brain cells gradually die.

Vascular dementia is usually the result of a stroke or series of strokes. A stroke blocks the flow of blood to the brain and so the brain does not receive enough oxygen and becomes damaged.

Dementia with Lewy bodies. Lewy bodies are abnormal spherical structures which develop in the nerve cells in the brain leading to the death of the cells.

Frontal lobe dementia. This is caused by the degeneration of one or both of the frontal lobes of the brain.

Early onset dementia. When people develop the disease before the age of 65 it is known as early onset, young onset or working age dementia. The symptoms are similar but the needs are usually different because of the lifestyles of younger people.

Some of the symptoms of dementia

Word Check 3

Check	✔	Meaning/translation
reasoning		
confused		
mood		
personality		
hallucinations		
apathetic		

Different types of dementia affect different parts of the brain.

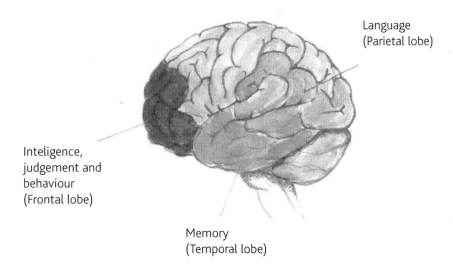

Language
(Parietal lobe)

Inteligence,
judgement and
behaviour
(Frontal lobe)

Memory
(Temporal lobe)

Figure 1.5 Different dementias

As a result there are varying symptoms. Below are some of the most common.

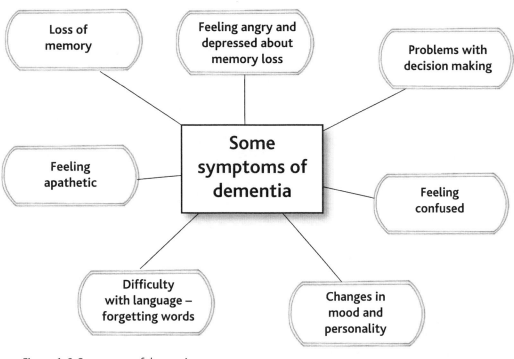

Loss of
memory

Feeling angry and
depressed about
memory loss

Problems with
decision making

Feeling
apathetic

**Some
symptoms of
dementia**

Feeling
confused

Difficulty
with language –
forgetting words

Changes in
mood and
personality

Figure 1.6 Symptoms of dementia

English Check 1

Choose a word from the vocabulary listed in Word Checks 1, 2 and 3 to fill in the spaces.

1 Memory loss is a _____ of dementia.

2 Dementia affects the _____ of the brain.

3 Because they keep forgetting, some people with dementia can become

angry, f_____ and sometimes depressed.

4 To _____ with someone means to be able to share someone's

feelings by imagining what it is like to be that person.

5 Vascular dementia can be a result of a _____

6 Even though it was her birthday party she did not join in – she was very

_____.

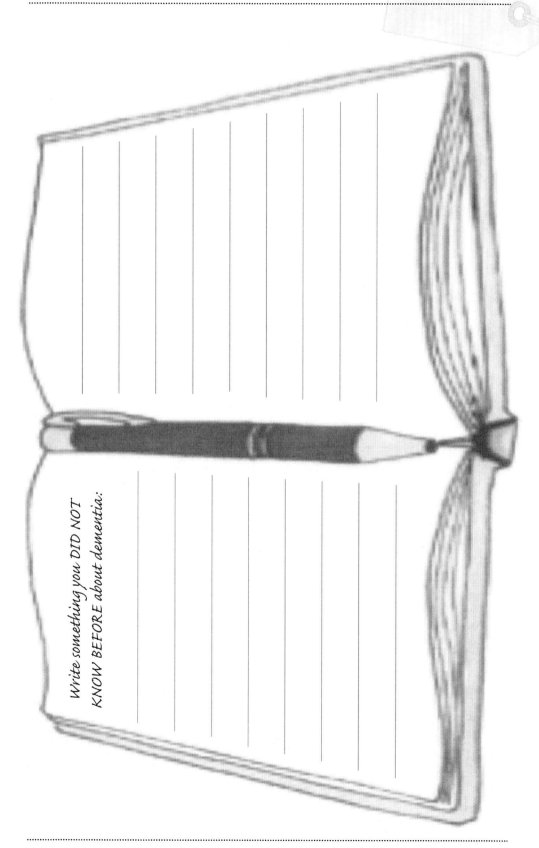

Write something you DID NOT KNOW BEFORE about dementia:

Current thinking about how to care for and how to treat people with dementia

Word Check 4

Check	✔	Meaning/translation
unique		
concepts		
approaches		
triggers		
rights		
model		
appropriate		

The care of the elderly and people with dementia in the UK may be different from the care in your country. It is important you understand these approaches as many of them are based on the legal rights of the person with dementia. Also your colleagues will usually think this way and you may lose their respect if you don't observe these methods. Basic training will usually be given to you to help you understand them.

You will hear many terms relating to these approaches – person-centred, personhood, equality, diversity, inclusion, rights, medical and social model of dementia. Each of these is explained below.

Person-centred approach

The carer who uses the person-centred approach believes in the following.

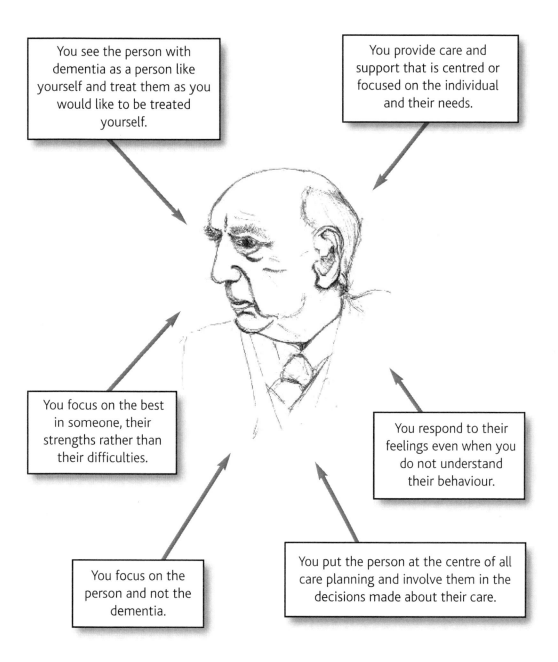

You see the person with dementia as a person like yourself and treat them as you would like to be treated yourself.

You provide care and support that is centred or focused on the individual and their needs.

You focus on the best in someone, their strengths rather than their difficulties.

You respond to their feelings even when you do not understand their behaviour.

You focus on the person and not the dementia.

You put the person at the centre of all care planning and involve them in the decisions made about their care.

Figure 1.7 Person-centred approach

These show in the day-to-day behaviour of the carer. They will:

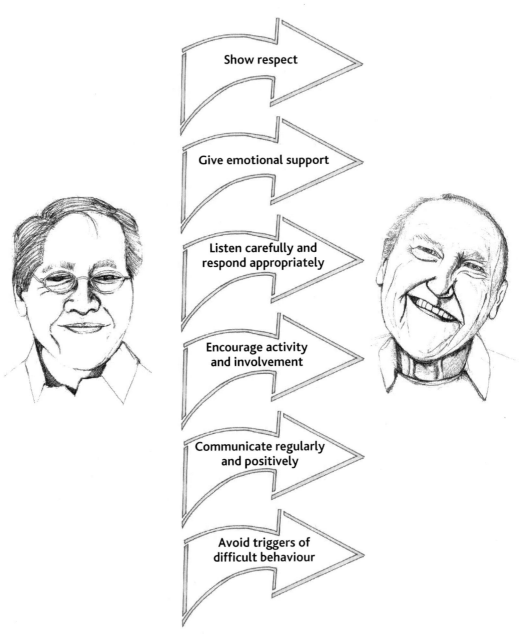

Show respect

Give emotional support

Listen carefully and respond appropriately

Encourage activity and involvement

Communicate regularly and positively

Avoid triggers of difficult behaviour

Figure 1.8 How the carer with a person-centred approach treats the person with dementia

For more information on the person-centred approach read the factsheet available at:

www.careuklearningdisabilities.com/uploads/pdf/Factsheet_person_centred_planning.pdf

Personhood

Personhood is another word you may hear. 'Personhood' is how a person is seen or thought of by others. A person with dementia will keep their 'personhood' if they are treated with respect and dignity; if they are seen as a person and not just as a dementia sufferer. Within person-centred care, the personhood of the person with dementia can be maintained by how they are treated, how they are spoken to and how they are regarded. As a carer you can recognise that this is very important to your own self-esteem, self-confidence and well-being. So it is with the person with dementia.

Equality, diversity, inclusion, rights

Equality ⟶ This is about treating people well and fairly. It does not mean treating everyone in the same way but understanding that people have different needs and these needs are met in different ways.

Diversity ⟶ Each person is unique with their own differences. These differences should be recognised and accepted.

Inclusion ⟶ This means accepting and including all people and their differences. All should have equal access and opportunities and no differences should stop this.

Rights ⟶ It is important to remember that ALL people have basic human rights. Part of the person-centred approach to care is to ensure that the person you are caring for has these rights! YOU have them – make sure the person you are caring for has them!

These concepts of equality, diversity, inclusion and rights are basic and necessary to a person-centred approach to care.

Medical and social models of dementia

When we talk about these models of dementia we are talking about how people view dementia – how they see it, what they think about it.

How we view dementia and how we view the person will affect how the person is treated.

The medical model of dementia	**Result**	Looking at people using the medical model can result in the doctors, nurses and care staff seeing and treating the symptoms and not seeing the person. The personhood of the individual may be ignored.
People see the disease before they see the person. They see what the damage to the brain has caused and view all behaviour as a result of the disease.		

The social model of dementia	**Result**	The person is at the centre of the planning. The needs of the person are seen as central. The person is shown respect and personhood is maintained longer. The greater the activity and social involvement of the person with dementia, the slower the disease will progress.
This is about looking at the person rather than the medical condition. This approach is what person-centred care is all about. Dementia is not just about the medical side but how it affects the way that the person with dementia interacts with other people, how they are viewed and how they are treated – that is '**personhood**'.		

English Check 2

1 Diversity is about recognising and accepting people's _____.

2 Inclusion is about people having the same _____ and that their differences should not affect this.

3 Using the social model of dementia is necessary for_____ _____ care.

4 Explain 'personhood' in your own words.

_____

_____

_____

_____

_____

_____

_____

_____

_____

_____

_____

_____

_____

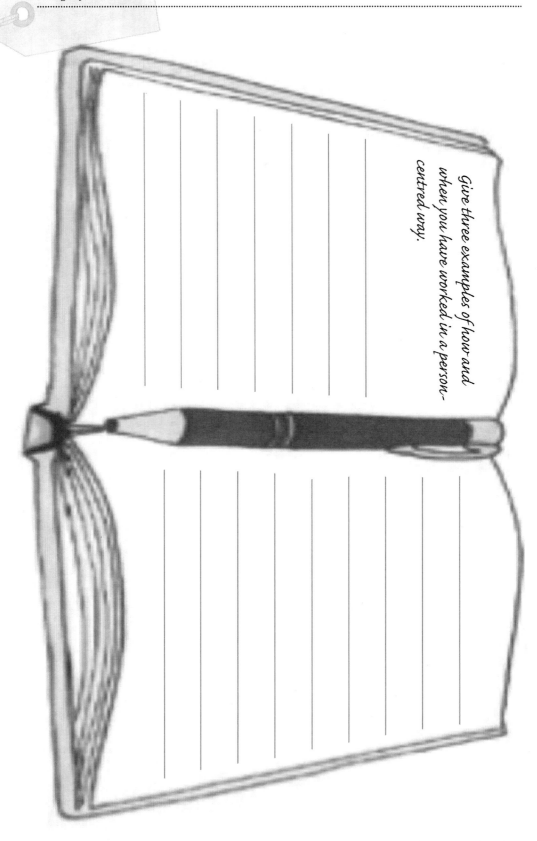

Give three examples of how and when you have worked in a person-centred way.

Part 2

Communication
– How do I get through?

"*Give us time to speak. Wait for us to search around that untidy heap on the floor of the brain for the word we want to use. Try not to finish our sentences. Just listen, and don't let us feel embarrassed if we lose the thread of what we say. Don't rush us into something because we can't think or speak fast enough to let you know whether we agree. Try to give us time to respond and to let you know whether we really want to do it.*"

Words of advice from Christine Bryden – a dementia sufferer

(Source: Better Health Channel – State Government of Victoria © 2013)

Word Check 5

Check	✓	Meaning/translation
dignity		
self-esteem		
verbally		
posture		
gesture		

There has been a lot of work, research and debate on the subject of communicating with people with dementia. This book does not intend to develop these ideas fully or attempt to deal in depth with the debate on communication. However, there are several points we can consider.

What is believed by most people who study communicating with people with dementia is that some level of communication is always possible – **you have to believe you can communicate**.

> *'It does seem that the opportunities for communicating depend to a large extent upon the belief of the person without dementia that communication is possible.'*
>
> **(Goldsmith, 1996, p.63)**

Of course, communication gets more and more difficult as the dementia progresses. Communicating with people in the early stages of dementia is completely different from communicating with someone in the later stages of dementia. You need a different approach, different skills.

To communicate effectively needs patience, time and skill. This book is based on believing that some level of communication is always possible, and aims to give help on basic communication skills and to provide some of the language you can use.

What is involved in communication?

Not being able to communicate can be one of the most frustrating and difficult problems for a person with dementia and also for their family and carers. As the illness progresses the person with dementia finds it more and more difficult to communicate verbally and to understand what others are saying. Imagine what this must be like!

There are many parts to communication and it is important that the carer is aware of all of them to be able to communicate effectively with a person with dementia. Did you know that communication is made up of three parts?

Communication

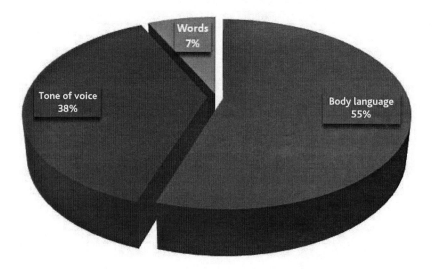

Figure 2.1 What is involved in communication?

Look at the percentages! The words we say are the smallest part of communication!

Look at body language and voice tone and pitch. These are always important but even more so when communicating with people in later stages of dementia. Even if they cannot speak, they usually understand body language, voice tone and touch.

Basic preparation

Before we look more closely at what is involved in good communication it is important to check and prepare some basics.

Check sight and hearing → If glasses or a hearing aid are used then check they are working correctly and also that the glasses are cleaned regularly.

Caring attitude → People with dementia may not understand what is being said but they still have feelings and emotions, they can usually understand body language and voice tone. Be respectful. Where appropriate, use touch to keep the person's attention and to communicate feelings of warmth and affection. Remember to keep body language positive and supportive.

Check the environment → Avoid background noises, such as TV or radio. Is the person comfortable?

Keep regular routines → It helps to reduce confusion if everyone uses the same daily routines and the same style of communication.

Tips for communicating with people with dementia

A person with dementia will read your body language and get information from your voice tone and facial expressions. As the dementia progresses and verbal communication becomes more difficult, your body language, tone of voice and the language you use will all become more important. For example, sudden movements, an angry voice or a tense facial expression may cause upset or distress and can make communication more difficult.

Making a start

- Always approach the person from the front.

- Be on the same eye-to-eye level.

- Identify yourself.

- Call the person by name.

Figure 2.2 Good communication

Below is a simplified checklist to consider when speaking to a person with dementia.

Dos	Don'ts
Smile.	Don't talk too fast. It confuses them.
Be calm and patient.	Don't argue with them – it only makes things worse.
Speak slowly and clearly.	
Make eye contact when you are talking.	Don't order the person around.
Make sentences short and simple.	Don't talk about them in front of them as though they are not there.
Focus on one idea at a time.	
Allow plenty of time to be understood.	Avoid background noise – turn off the TV.
Give plenty of time for a response.	Don't keep telling them what they can't do – instead tell them what they can do.
Use touch (if appropriate) to hold attention and reassure.	Don't ask a lot of questions that rely on good memory.
Give visual cues. Point or touch the item you want the individual to use. Or begin the task for the person to show them how to do it.	When asking questions, don't ask 'why' questions. Use 'what', 'when', 'who', and so on.

Table 2.1 Dos and Don'ts when speaking to a person with dementia.
Based on Tan (2010)

To get more information on communicating with a person with dementia read the Alzheimer's Association brochure, available at:

www.alz.org/national/documents/brochure_communication.pdf

Have a conversation with one of your patients/clients. Use the list above and make notes on what you did and did not say/do.

Listening

Listening is a very important part of communicating. It must be active listening – not just pretending to listen or only 'half listening'.

> That's really interesting.

> Tell me more about that.

> You must have enjoyed that.

Listen carefully to what the person is saying. Show you are listening and give them plenty of encouragement.

> Take your time – there's no rush.

> Tell me how you feel.

When you haven't understood fully, don't pretend you have! Tell the person what you have understood and check with them to see if you are right.

> Did you mean you want to change your clothes?

> Did you say you wanted to watch TV? Is that right?

If the person is feeling sad, let them express their feelings. Sometimes the best thing to do is to just listen and show that you care.

Remember! Due to memory loss, some people won't remember things such as their medical history, family and friends. You will need to use your common sense and act appropriately around what they've said. For example, they might say that they have just eaten when you know they haven't.

Communicating with people in later stages of dementia

Symptoms of the later stages of dementia

Memory loss
Can be severe – for example, not recognising themselves in the mirror, not recognising close family or familiar objects, believing they are living at another time in their past.

→

Your response
Use your language of reassurance. Keep talking in a quiet gentle voice. Touch if appropriate. Take mirrors away if reflection is troubling. If they are in the past, talk to them about it. Don't argue. If they are talking about their mother – ask them about her.

Poor mobility
Walking and other tasks gradually become more difficult. They can easily fall, they will drop items and they will often bump into things.

→

Your response
Be watchful when they are moving about. Help them to sit or stand up. Accompany them when they are moving about.

Communication problems
Communication becomes very difficult. They may not be able to speak, they may use the wrong words, they may shout or cry out, and they may display very difficult or unusual behaviour.

→

Your response
Remember there are other ways of communicating than just speaking – body language, facial expressions and gestures are very important. Watch the person for clues about how they are feeling. Carry on talking. Don't presume they cannot understand. If they don't understand, you are still recognising their personhood, their dignity!

Weight loss
Many people will lose weight in the later stages of dementia as they eat less. This can cause them to become ill more frequently, fall more easily and generally be less able to cope.

Your response
Support them at meal times. Help them and encourage them to eat and drink.

Incontinence
This can have many causes – infection, medication or perhaps forgetting where the toilet is!

Your response
Be sensitive. Remember the dignity of the person. Use reassuring language. Imagine yourself in that situation!

Unusual behaviour
Go to Part 4 for a closer look at this topic

For further information see Alzheimer's Society, The Later Stages of Dementia, available at:

www.alzheimers.org.uk/site/scripts/documents_info.php?documentID=101

Validation

Validation is a term used by Kitwood (cited in De Bellis et al, 2009). It is from his list of 'positive person work'. He explains that it is about accepting that what the person with dementia is experiencing is real to them so the listener should accept this and respond with understanding. So, for example, if the person is upset about someone who is not there, perhaps a parent, then the carer should say they understand the upset and ask about the missing person.

> I understand how upset you are Harry. Tell me about your brother.

So validation means accepting what the person is saying and talking to the person about what they are feeling/seeing and not dismissing it as unimportant or 'It's just the dementia causing it.'

Knowing the person's past can often help with understanding what they are saying or how they are acting. In Part 4 of this book we talk about life histories, a useful tool in helping to understand behaviour in the present.

Examples

1

> John was constantly agitated, pacing the corridors and banging on windows and locked doors.

> **Past history**
> A passionate gardener, John wanted to go into the garden but could not explain this.

> It's OK John. We'll go out into the garden and see what needs doing.

So, the reason for John's behaviour was not the dementia but his frustration at not being able to garden – his life-long hobby.

2

Michael was constantly complaining about a leaky roof in his room – he would get very agitated.

Past history
His family told his carer that Michael had always had a fear of becoming incontinent.

Show me where the leak is Michael. Tell me when it next happens.

So, the reason for Michael's behaviour was not the dementia but his previous fear of incontinence.

3

Maggie was constantly folding, unfolding and tidying napkins in the dining room, mumbling under her breath.

Past history
In Maggie's life history it said that her mother had died when Maggie was quite young and she was left responsible for all the housework.

You've had a very busy life, Maggie. I bet you were always tidying up at home. Do you want to help me sort the cutlery?

So, the reason for Maggie's behaviour was not the dementia but a life of always being busy, a life she knew and wants to carry on with.

It is important to remember this – all behaviour has a reason. The dementia just causes the unusual behaviours when the person cannot express what they are feeling. There are many books and articles about this. Graham Stokes, in his book *And Still the Music Plays* (2010), writes lots of stories of dementia patients he has met and explains how their past histories impact on their current behaviour. Similar stories are in *The Validation Breakthrough* by Feil and de Klerk-Rubin (2012).

Here is a checklist for when communicating with people in the later stages of dementia.

Remember! Without speech, body language and voice tone are even more important.

· **Respond with kindness and reassurance**.

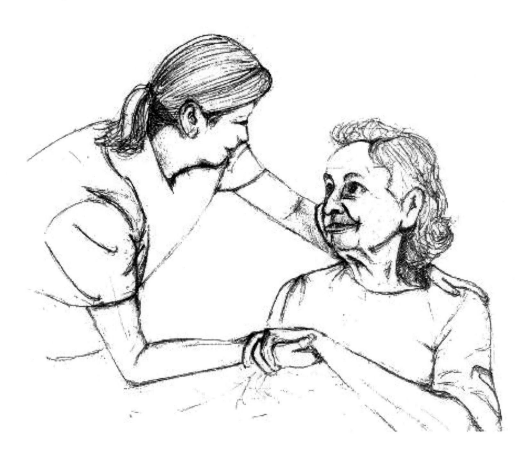

- **Position** – Stand or sit at the front of the person, at same level and with eye contact.

- **Speak** – Don't presume they do not understand just because they cannot respond.

- **Your voice** – Keep it calm, quiet and use the appropriate language.

- **Body language** – Always have positive facial expressions and a friendly body posture.

- **Touch** – If it is OK to touch the person, a comforting touch is very reassuring and also a way to keep attention.

- **Don't just blame their behaviour on the dementia.** This person is communicating. What are they trying to tell you? Remember! Validation!

- **Their reality** – Remember, if the person is confused or agitated, they believe the situation is true. Don't argue! Reassure and don't show anger or impatience.

- **Non-verbal clues** – Pay attention to their body language and facial expressions. Do they seem in pain, or frightened? Watch how they hold themselves and move about. All these may give you clues about how they are feeling and what they are trying to communicate.

- **Listen for clues** – Something they say may explain their behaviour.

At work: Make notes of when someone in the later stages of dementia was displaying difficult behaviour. Did you observe any non-verbal clues?

Advice from a person with dementia

Christine Bryden

Of course the best people to ask for advice are the people who are suffering from dementia itself. This is not always possible but, when it is, don't be afraid of asking for advice from them. Some dementia sufferers have written books about their life with the illness. One such person is Christine Bryden. She was diagnosed at the age of 46. She has written about ways family and carers can help a person with dementia. Christine is also the author of *Who Will I Be When I Die?*

Here are some of Christine's suggestions for communicating with a person with dementia.

Figure 2.3 Christine Bryden – a current sufferer of dementia.

- Give us time to speak. Wait for us to search around that untidy heap on the floor of the brain for the word we want to use. Try not to finish our sentences. Just listen, and don't let us feel embarrassed if we lose the thread of what we say.

- Don't rush us into something because we can't think or speak fast enough to let you know whether we agree. Try to give us time to respond and to let you know whether we really want to do it.

- When you want to talk to us, think of some way to do this without questions, which can alarm us or make us feel uncomfortable. If we have forgotten something special that happened recently, don't assume it wasn't special for us too. Just give us a gentle prompt – we may just be momentarily blank.

- Don't try too hard to help us remember something that just happened. If it never registered, we are never going to be able to recall it.

- Avoid background noise if you can. If the TV is on, mute it first.

- If children are underfoot, remember we will get tired very easily and find it very hard to concentrate on talking and listening as well. Maybe one child at a time and without background noise would be best.

- Earplugs may be useful if visiting shopping centres or other noisy places. (Source: Better Health Channel – State Government of Victoria © 2013)

For more about Christine Bryden go to her site: **www.christinebryden.com**

Part 3

Language
– What do I say?

> *When you want to talk to us, think of some way to do this without questions, which can alarm us or make us feel uncomfortable. If we have forgotten something special that happened recently, don't assume it wasn't special for us too. Just give us a gentle prompt – we may just be momentarily blank.*

Words of advice from Christine Bryden – a dementia sufferer
(Source: Better Health Channel – State Government of Victoria © 2013).

Word Check 6

Check	✓	Meaning/translation
sincere		
priorities		
compassion		
reassure		
acknowledge		
to be valued		
concern		
praise		
persuade		
optimism		
suggest		

General language used when dealing with people with dementia

It is very important to remember that caring is not just about washing, dressing, feeding, and so on. Yes, these are important and necessary but they are only a part of caring.

Remember! Personhood! The person you are caring for has feelings like yourself, has had lots of experiences and has a whole range of needs, wishes and priorities. They deserve to be treated with respect and dignity. Being fed, washed and put to bed are not particularly dignified experiences, but they can be made a lot more acceptable by good communication; communication that shows compassion, empathy, concern, respect, encouragement and reassurance.

Epp (2003) cites Kitwood who said that good dementia care should aim to keep the personhood even though mental powers are failing.

Remember! People with dementia have communication problems which become worse as their illness progresses. As it becomes more difficult for them to communicate they may communicate using challenging behaviour. **All behaviour is a means of communication**.

As you will see in Part 4, there is a wide range of possible difficult behaviour from people with dementia. When dealing with these situations you need to use a range of functional English – that is language used for a specific purpose. In these situations we need the correct language to:

- show respect and patience

- calm the person

- show concern and reassure

- encourage and praise to build self-esteem

- make suggestions and persuade.

All of this should be delivered in simple, matter-of-fact English. This section will give you useful language to help you to cope in these situations.

Remember! From Part 2 on communication.

- Check the environment.

- Use positive body language.

- When speaking:

  – remain calm and talk in a gentle, matter-of-fact way

  – keep sentences short and simple, focusing on one idea at a time

  – always allow plenty of time for what you have said to be understood

  – sign post! Let them know what you are going to talk about. It can be helpful to use orienting names or labels whenever you can, such as 'your son Jack', or 'The TV programme you're watching ...'

— you may need to use some hand gestures and facial expressions to make yourself understood. Pointing or demonstrating can help. Touching and holding the person's hand may help keep their attention and show them that you care.

Showing respect and patience

Why? When you show respect to someone you are acknowledging that they are important to you. This is a basic need everyone has – to be valued. You may not always agree with what they say, but you must always respect that they have a right to their views.

How? There are several simple things you should make sure you do.

- Listen carefully to what they are saying. Make eye contact with them as this is the best way to show interest.

- Be fair – don't judge them unfairly because of their views or behaviour.

- Give them time to say what it is they want to say.

- Be sensitive to their thoughts and feelings.

- Make the person know you value their opinion.

- Don't seem uninterested or bored at all.

Showing concern

Why? When a person is upset or sad you can make them feel better if they know you are concerned about them.

How? There are many things you can say to show concern. Some of them are on the next page.

Remember!

When someone with dementia is confused, don't argue or contradict them. Remember it's their reality.

English Check 3

Now you try it out.

What would you say in the following situations?

1 You see Mary sitting by the window crying.

You:

_____

Mary: My leg is hurting.

You:

_____

2 Harry is sitting alone shouting loudly and shaking his fist.

You:

_____

Harry: It's my neighbour's dog – it's in my garden again!

You:

_____

Comforting

Why? Everyone needs 'a shoulder to cry on' sometimes. It is natural to want comfort in times of unhappiness. People with dementia may be upset because of their frustration at their symptoms or for reasons that are not real. **But** – the situation is real for them!

How? Comfort by listening patiently and wait until they have finished talking. Do not judge, complain or get annoyed. The comfort of touch is very strong if appropriate – a hand on the shoulder, a hug.

Words of comfort:

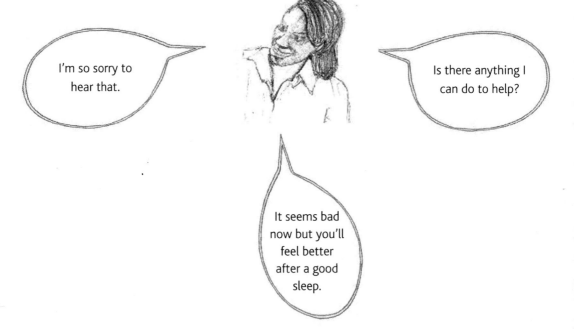

I'm so sorry to hear that.

Is there anything I can do to help?

It seems bad now but you'll feel better after a good sleep.

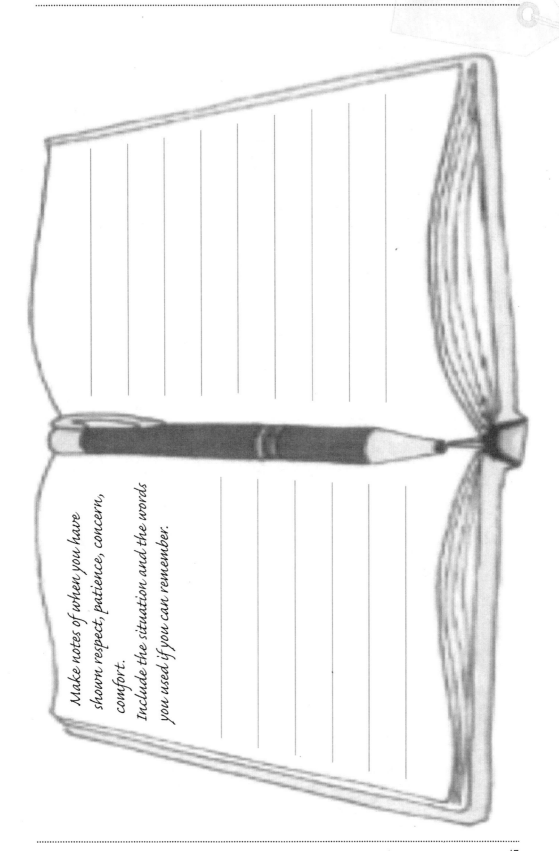

Make notes of when you have shown respect, patience, concern, comfort.
Include the situation and the words you used if you can remember.

Calming and reassuring

Why? People with dementia can get agitated, angry or very fearful. You may not understand the reason but in the mind of the person the reasons are very real. Be patient and try to calm and reassure them.

How? Apart from the words you use you also need to show positive and supportive body language as well as a calm and soothing voice. Be careful of intonation and stress in your voice.

Ask what the problem is – 'Why are you so upset?' – then listen carefully.

Don't worry.

You'll be fine/It'll be fine.

There's no need to worry.

There's nothing to worry about.

It isn't as bad as all that.

Whatever you may have heard, it isn't true. You probably misunderstood ....

English Check 4

Now you have a go.

1 Anne is crying and obviously very upset about something.

You:

_____

Anne: My sister is very ill. She was coming to visit tomorrow but she doesn't know when she can come now.

You:

_____

2 Hilda is alone in her room, crying and shouting.

You:

_____

Hilda: There's someone banging on my window. They want to get in.

You:

_____

Suggesting and advising

Why? Again you need to remember that people with dementia still need to be offered choices and to have things suggested rather than to be told or ordered to do something.

How? You can use the following phrases to either suggest or advise.

English Check 5

Let's practise.

Put the correct word or phrase into the gap.

1 Why _____ go to the lounge?

don't we / don't we to / don't

2 Let's _____ for a walk.

to go out / going out / go out

3 How about _____ this afternoon?

to tidy / tidy / tidying your room

4 Why _____ watch TV tonight?

don't go / don't you / not you go

5 _____ to the activity club this afternoon.

Let's going / Let's to go / Let's go

6 What _____ Mary for help?

about asking / about to ask / about ask

7 How _____ into the garden for some fresh air?

about going / about to go / about you going

Persuading

Why? To persuade someone means to make someone decide to do something, especially by giving them reasons why they should do it, or asking them many times to do it. People with dementia often need persuading as they can be apathetic or find decision making difficult.

How? You can use the phrases of suggesting and advising then add a reason. For example, 'If I were you I'd put on a warm jumper, it's really cold today' or 'Let's watch TV – there's a very interesting programme on.'

Your voice and body are your best helpers.

1 Body language – make sure that you have a positive posture. If your shoulders are sagging and your legs are crossed you won't seem interested or sincere.

2 Your voice – a calm, gentle voice will be more persuasive. Sound interesting by making your voice go up and down. Don't speak too quickly and give time for what you say to be taken in.

Some persuasive words and phrases you can use.

Let's go down to the dining room. *I'm sure* you must be really hungry.

We ought to go down to the dining room. Dinner will be getting cold.

I think it's a good idea to go down to the dining room now. Dinner will be getting cold.

I think we should go down to the dining room now, you must be starving.

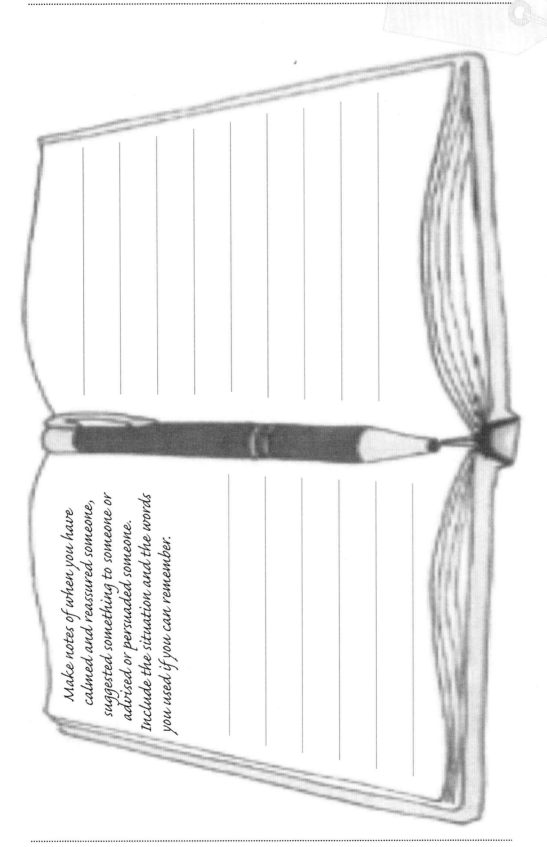

Make notes of when you have calmed and reassured someone, suggested something to someone or advised or persuaded someone. Include the situation and the words you used if you can remember.

Praising

Why? Everyone likes to be praised. It raises self-esteem and confidence to know we are good at something, we have done well, or we have succeeded in something we have attempted. This is obviously even more beneficial to someone who is experiencing the frustrations of dementia.

How? Here are some useful phrases.

I don't know how you do it, it's fantastic.

You've done a brilliant job!

Well done!

You don't mean to say you did that without any help?

That's fantastic / excellent / brilliant!

Encouraging

Why? Everyone likes to be encouraged. This is more important with dementia patients who may be experiencing apathy or depression and feeling frustrated at losing their skills in several areas.

How? Here are some useful phrases.

Come on, you can do it.

That's a real improvement.

You're coming along (really) well!

Keep up the good work.

Keep going.

You're on the right lines.

(Used to say someone is not exactly right but could get it right if they tried again.)

Language of optimism/cheering up

Why? Often dementia patients feel a bit down or unhappy. This can be due to the obvious frustrations of the illness or it could be something not real – but remember it is real to the person with dementia!

How? Here are some phrases you can use to try to make them feel better.

Smile!

Never mind – it's the outing tomorrow – that will make you feel better.

Come on, cheer up. What would you like to do? Play cards?

It's not the end of the world.

Every cloud has a silver lining

Never mind – tomorrow you'll be seeing your son.

(Used when something positive can be said when something unpleasant has happened. Every bad situation has some good aspect to it. For example, 'I'm afraid the trip has been cancelled – but that means your daughter can visit you. Every cloud has a silver lining'.)

Now you have a go.

English Check 6

1 Christine is struggling with her shoe laces and getting very frustrated.

You: _____

Christine finally manages to tie them.

You: _____

2 Henry won't go down for dinner. He says it's too cold in the dining room.

You: _____

3 Thomas is sitting in the lounge looking very miserable.

You: _____

Thomas: I don't know – I just feel sad.

You: _____

Make notes of when you have praised, encouraged or cheered someone up. Include the situation and the words you used if you can remember.

Part 4

Challenging behaviour
– How do I react?

The body, it crumbles, grace and vigour depart,

There is now a stone where I once had a heart.

But inside this old carcass a young girl still dwells,

And now and again my battered heart swells.

I remember the joys, I remember the pain,

And I'm loving and living life over again.

I think of the years ... all too few, gone too fast,

And accept the stark fact that nothing can last.

So open your eyes, nurses, open and see,

... Not a crabby old woman; look closer ... see ME!!

('An Old Woman's Poem' – Anonymous. For complete poem see Appendix 1.)

Figure 4.1 The thoughts of a person with dementia

Word Check 7

Check	✓	*Meaning/translation*
accommodate		
belittle		
fidget		
flexibility		
tackle		
anxious		
humiliate		
inhibitions		
intensify		
out of the blue		
criticise		
disorientated		

Check yourself first!

As well as looking at the challenging behaviour of the person with dementia, it is also very important you look at your own behaviour. Your behaviour can affect the person with dementia and even make things worse or trigger their challenging behaviour.

Check the following.

• Are you calm and not feeling annoyed or angry? If you are feeling annoyed, take a deep breath and remember – don't take it personally.

- Are you showing positive body language and reassuring facial expression?

- Is your voice at the right pitch?

- Are you facing the person and at eye level?

- Do they know who you are?

- Is the environment as calm as possible?

Handling challenging behaviour

Some of the most difficult challenges of caring for a person with dementia are the personality and behaviour changes that often occur. You can best deal with these challenges by using creativity, flexibility, patience and compassion.

The following are tips to help you cope with any unusual behaviours.

- The person cannot help their behaviour. It is not done deliberately. Their reason and logic are quite different from yours.

- Is the problem a real difficulty? If they don't want to get dressed now, do they need to? Could you wait until they are calmer? If they want to sleep on the floor, could the mattress be moved to allow that?

- Behaviour is a form of communication. What are they trying to tell you?

- Behaviour is triggered. Did you notice what happened just before the behaviour?

- Be calm, reassure them, comfort them.

- Distract them. Massage the hand, play calming music for example. You may need to change your response. Dementia progresses, so what calmed them yesterday may not calm them today.

- Some of the behaviours you may find very irritating. If you feel you are 'losing it', leave the room, if possible, and come back later. If not possible, take deep breaths, try to relax and remember they can't help it!

- Don't be afraid to ask for help – from colleagues, your manager, the family or organisations.

(Adapted from Alzheimer's Society, *Unusual Behaviour*: **www.alzheimers.org.uk/site/scripts/documents.php?categoryID=200357**)

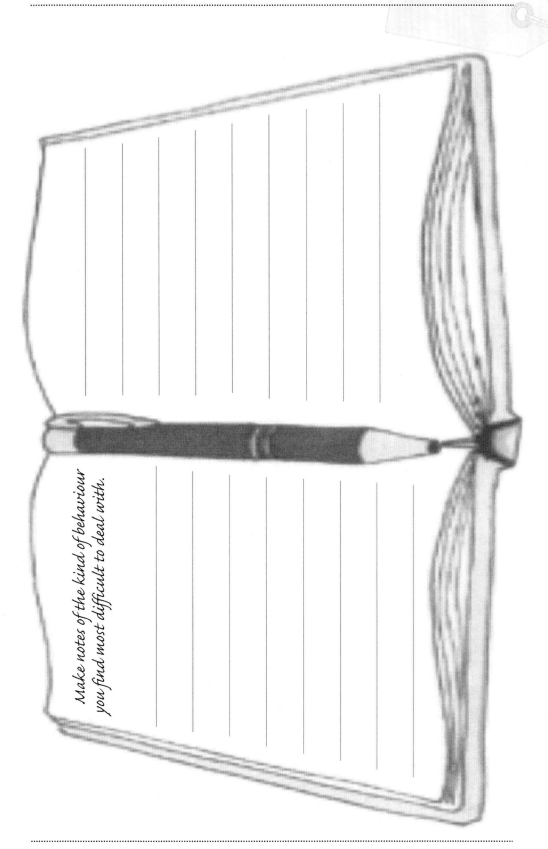

Make notes of the kind of behaviour you find most difficult to deal with.

The most common dementia-associated behaviours

The following is an overview of the most common dementia-associated behaviours with suggestions for what to do that may be useful!

In almost all situations you need to use the language we have looked at – calming, encouraging and persuasive language, showing respect and concern.

Check you know the meaning of each word in the list below – some of the more difficult words are in the Word Check section at the back of the book. Make a note of any meanings you didn't know.

Confused

Agitation

Hallucinations

Aggression

Repetitive behaviour

Shouting and screaming

Lack of inhibition

Night-time waking

Trailing and checking

Hiding and losing things

Restlessness

Suspicion

Apathy

Sundowning

Wandering

> **Remember! Behaviour is a form of communication. What is the person trying to communicate?**

Triggers

Finding out or observing triggers is extremely important as it can indicate why the trigger has caused the behaviour and can also enable you to avoid them in the future. We will therefore take time to look more closely at this topic.

Work out what triggers the aggressive behaviour

Think about all the times when the person has become aggressive, agitated or confused. What happened before their outbursts? Can you identify any common triggers? This could give you a clue as to what is troubling the person. Use the list below to give you some ideas.

People with dementia may become aggressive, agitated or confused in the following circumstances.

They feel frustrated, stressed or humiliated because they are no longer able to cope with the everyday demands of life.

➡

Your response
Don't be angry or annoyed and hide any irritation that you feel. Avoid situations where the person is likely to fail. Praise any achievements, and remind them about things that they can still do, rather than what they cannot.

They feel that their independence or privacy is threatened. Being forced to accept help with personal things such as washing, dressing or going to the toilet can be stressful as all their life this has been a private thing.

➡

Your response
Find tactful ways to offer help without seeming to take over. Help them to do as much for themselves as possible. Be sensitive. Imagine yourself in that situation.

They feel they are in trouble because they have forgotten something or have made a mistake when doing something.

→

Your response
Try to remember that the person may not understand what you are trying to do and why. Wherever possible, explain things calmly and in simple sentences. Keep the tone of your voice calm and reassuring. Break tasks down into easy steps, so that they can do as much as possible for themselves.

They feel confused or anxious because there is too much noise, too many people, or too much change in routine.

→

Your response
If the person does not seem to be coping well, take them to a quieter place. Make sure they have a calm and stress-free routine.

They feel nervous or frightened because they don't recognise where they are or who they are with.

→

Your response
Speak calmly. Tell them where they are or who the person is. Comfort them.

They are frightened by a sudden noise, maybe a loud voice, sudden movements or a person approaching them from behind without warning.

→

Your response
Comfort and calm them – remember appropriate touching can be helpful. Explain simply what the cause of the fear was.

They are in pain, they are bored, or perhaps just thirsty.

→

Your response
Check the possible causes of the pain. If they are bored then find activities to stimulate the person's interest, and make sure that they take enough physical exercise. For more information on activities go to Part 5 of the book.

(Alzheimer's Society, *Dealing with Aggressive Behaviour:*
www.alzheimers.org.uk/site/scripts/documents_info.php?documentID=96)

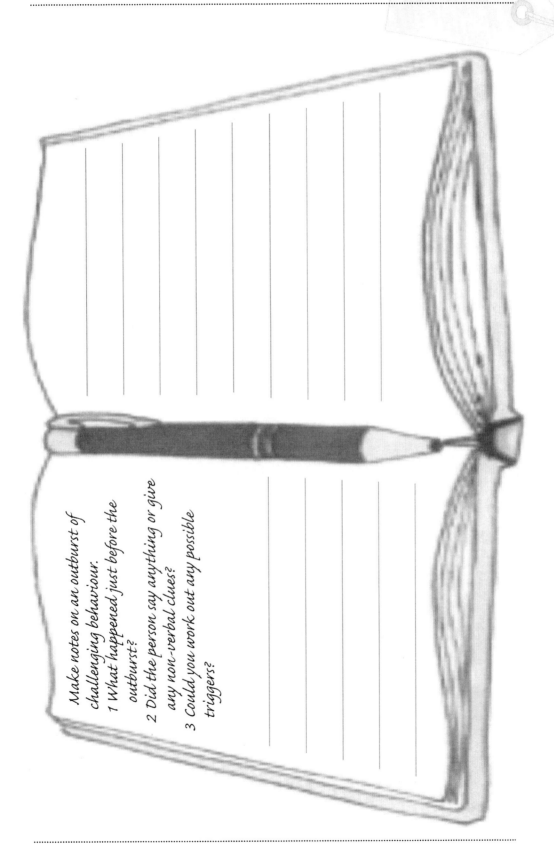

Make notes on an outburst of challenging behaviour.
1 What happened just before the outburst?
2 Did the person say anything or give any non-verbal clues?
3 Could you work out any possible triggers?

The following pages look at each example of challenging or unusual behaviour in turn.

Information has been taken from different sources with kind permission from the following.

MentalHelp.net. *Tips for Dealing with Specific Dementia Problematic Behaviors:*
www.mentalhelp.net/poc/view_doc.php?type=doc&id=15346

Alzhiemer's Society. *Dealing with Aggressive Behaviour:*
www.alzheimers.org.uk/site/scripts/documents_info.php?documentID=96

Alzheimer's Society. *Unusual Behaviour:*
www.alzheimers.org.uk/site/scripts/documents.php?categoryID=200357

Confusion

What is it?

Dementia patients often experience confusion. They become confused about people, places and time. The person may still know who they themselves are, but may not recognise others and where they are, the time, the date or the year. They may think they are somewhere else or in a different time, perhaps thinking they are young and at home. They may also become confused about objects and what they are for, such as forks or pens.

What to say

'It's your brother, Tony.'

'Here's your pen for writing your letter.'

'I'm Edgar, your carer. I'm here to help you.'

'Don't worry. You are safe here.'

Possible causes

Causes can be linked to the normal process of ageing. Further causes could be poor nutrition, medication side effects, infections, strokes, depression and several others.

What to do

Remember, to the person with dementia it is real. Don't argue with them. Give simple, clear statements about the situation. If they say, for example, 'My mother is in the kitchen and she is angry with me,' rather than disputing this, say something like, 'What was your mother like?' or 'I bet your mother was often in the kitchen.'

When common objects are confused provide simple, clear, positive answers when the person needs help. For example, if the person seems confused about the purpose of a pen, simply say, 'Here's your pen for writing your letter.' You could also calmly show the person how to use the utensil (e.g. by saying 'watch me').

Never be angry with the person or talk to them in a belittling way for becoming confused!

Agitation

What is it?
People with dementia often become restless, anxious or upset.

What to say
Reassure, calm, comfort the person.
Remember your phrases – for example,
'Don't worry!', 'Is there anything I can do to
help?', 'I know how you are feeling.'

Possible causes
- Pain or discomfort – for example, being too hot, too cold, hungry, needing to go to the toilet.
- Being frustrated about something.
- Being overexcited or overstimulated.

What to do

- Note any triggers and listen to the person for clues to causes.
- Check your body language. Is your voice calm?
- Reduce noise, clutter or the number of people in the room.
- Try gentle touch, soothing music, reading or walks. Speak in a reassuring voice.
- Keep dangerous objects out of reach.
- Allow the person to do as much for themselves as possible.
- Talk calmly to them. Tell them you understand their frustration.
- Distract the person with a snack or an activity.
- Don't go on about the incident. Try to let them forget it. Confronting a confused person may increase anxiety.

Hallucinations

What are they?
Hallucinations are sensory experiences that seem real, but are not. The most common hallucinations are seeing or hearing something that is not really there. Hallucinations can also occur in regard to taste, smell and touch.

What to say
'Don't worry, it's just the wind in the trees.'
'You're safe here with me.'
'It's just a shadow from the light.'

Possible causes
- Progression of the dementia.
- Medication.
- Eyesight problems.

What to do

Because hallucinations seem real to those with dementia do not try to convince the person that they are imagining things. Instead, recognise the person's feelings; reassure the person that you are there to help. State simply and calmly how you see the situation, but avoid arguing or trying to convince the person they are wrong. Offer reassurance and a simple explanation – for example, the curtains move because of a draught from the window, the loud noise was a plane going overhead. Redirect the person to a pleasant activity. Also consider whether the hallucination is actually bothersome. If it is a 'nice' hallucination (e.g. seeing a pretty orchard outside that is not really there), there may be no benefit in trying to discourage it.

Aggression

What is it?

People with dementia may sometimes behave aggressively in different ways: being verbally abusive, kicking or pinching, lashing out, getting too upset about something that is really quite trivial.

What to say

You will need to remember all your phrases for calming and reassuring here.

Possible causes

- Feeling frightened or humiliated.

- Feeling frustrated at being unable to understand others or make themselves understood.

- The physical effects of dementia, which may have damaged their judgement and self-control.

- Losing the knowledge of what acceptable behaviour is.

What to do

Dealing with aggressive behaviour is not easy, and there are no simple answers.

- Stay calm, use a reassuring tone of voice and remember positive body language.

- Try to identify what triggers the aggression.

- Reassure the person, and acknowledge that you can see they are upset.

- Try to distract their attention.

- Ask yourself if whatever you are trying to do for the person really needs to be done at that moment. You may be able to avoid a confrontation if you come back later.

- If you need to, call for help.

Key tip: don't take it personally

Any form of aggression can be upsetting, but the most important thing to remember is that the person cannot help it. You may feel the aggression is about you but actually it is probably that you were there at the time!

You have a go!

1 Harry is sitting alone and looking confused. He has a piece of paper in his hand with a telephone number on it. He says it's his mother's number and he wants to call her. You know she died many years ago.

What do you say/do?

2 Mary is screaming in her bedroom. She says someone is coming through the window. The curtains are open, it's windy and there is a tree outside.

What do you say/do?

3 Tom has been trying to tell you something, you know it's something about his brother but his speech is poor and you can't understand him. He starts to shout and becomes aggressive.

What do you say/do?

Repetitive behaviour

What is it?

People with dementia often repeat a word, question, or action over and over again (e.g. saying 'What are we doing today?'). This behaviour is usually harmless, but it can be very annoying for those who are caring for the person.

What to say

'Do you want to help me sort out these newspapers?'

'Shall we tidy your sock drawer?'

Possible causes

Repetitive behaviour is usually a sign of insecurity, since people with dementia are often looking for something comfortable and familiar or something over which they have some degree of control.

What to do

Look to see if there was a trigger. If you recognise the cause it can help you to respond better. If the repetition is an action, try turning it into an activity that makes the person feel useful. For example, if the person is constantly fidgeting with their hands, try giving them some socks to sort or some ornaments to clean.

Shouting and screaming

> **What is it?**
> The person may continually call out for someone, shout the same word or scream over and over again.

> **What to say**
> Use your calming, comforting and reassuring phrases here.

> **Possible causes**
> - They could be in pain or ill.
> - They may be having hallucinations.
> - They may feel lonely or distressed.
> - If their short-term memory is damaged they may not remember that you are in the next room and believe they are alone.
> - They may feel anxious about their failing memory.
> - They may be feeling bored.
> - They may feel stressed by too much noise and bustle.

What to do

If the person shouts out at night, a nightlight in the bedroom may be comforting. Consider how the room looks in the dark. Are there shadows or shapes that cannot be seen when the light is on but that could look frightening in the dark?

If they are calling for someone from their past, try talking to them about this time in their life and be comforting. Avoid unhappy facts that may cause distress – if the person they are asking for has died, they may not remember this fact and will feel they are hearing it for the first time.

Lack of inhibition

What is it?

The person may behave in a way that other people find embarrassing. Some people with dementia may undress in public or stroke or expose their genitals in public. Sometimes they may lift their skirt or fiddle with trouser fasteners. Sometimes it's rude behaviour – for example, insulting people or swearing or spitting.

What to say

'Come with me to your room – it's more comfortable there.'

'Shall we go into the lounge to see what's going on?'

'Let's see if there is anything on TV.'

Possible causes

This is because of their failing memory and general confusion. In a few cases, this may be due to specific damage to the brain.

What to do

Try to react calmly.

- When undressing in public, they have probably forgotten when and where it is appropriate to remove their clothes. If this happens, take the person somewhere private, and check whether they are too hot or are uncomfortable or want to use the toilet.

- Inappropriate sexual behaviour may be because they have forgotten what is acceptable social behaviour. If this happens, try to distract their attention. It is important to remember that having dementia does not mean a person no longer has physical or sexual needs – simply that inhibitions and social skills may not be functioning.

- Some actions, such as lifting a skirt or fiddling with trouser fasteners, may not be related to sex at all – it may simply be a sign that the person wants to use the toilet.

- If the person behaves rudely, don't argue or try to correct the behaviour. Try to distract them, and explain to other people later that the behaviour is due to dementia.

Night-time waking

What is it?
Many people with dementia are restless at night and find it difficult to sleep.

What to say
'It's really late, everyone's asleep. You should go back to bed, you'll be shattered tomorrow.'

Possible causes
Older people often need less sleep than younger people in any case. Dementia can affect people's body clocks so that they may get up in the night, get dressed or even go outside.

What to do

- Make sure the person has enough exercise during the day and that they use the toilet before bed.

- Try a walk before bedtime if possible, a warm milky drink and soothing company before they fall asleep.

- If the person wakes up, gently remind them that it is night-time.

- During the light summer months it can feel like daytime even late at night or very early in the morning, so put a clock that shows whether it is am or pm next to the bed and, if possible, use darker curtains or blackout blinds.

You have a go!

1 Helen is constantly folding then unfolding her handkerchief.

What can you say/do?

2   Henry is shouting constantly in his bedroom. He is rubbing his head and
    trying to pull his pyjamas off.

    What can you say/do?

3 Albert keeps scratching his groin. He is mumbling to himself and then tries to take his trousers off. He is in the lounge.

What do you say/do?

Trailing and checking

What is it?

The person constantly follows their carers or loved ones around, or calls out to check where they are.

What to say

Use your calming and reassuring phrases.

Distract them:

'Would you like to do more of your scrap book?'

'What about playing a game?'

Possible causes

Living with dementia makes many people feel extremely insecure and anxious. A few moments may seem like hours to a person with dementia, and they may only feel safe if other people are nearby.

What to do

This behaviour can be very difficult to cope with, but try not to show you are annoyed.

If you are busy, give the person something to do – a task or activity, or put the TV or radio on.

Go to 'Activities' in Part 5 for some ideas.

Hiding and losing things

What is it?

People with dementia sometimes hide things and then forget where they are – or forget that they have hidden them at all.

What to say

'I'm sure it's around here somewhere.'

'It can't be far.'

'Don't worry, we'll soon find it.'

Possible causes

The wish to hide things may be due to feelings of insecurity and a desire to hold on to what little the person still has.

What to do

- However impatient you feel, try to be reassuring.

- Don't leave anything important lying around.

- Try to find out the person's hiding places so that you can tactfully help find 'missing' items.

- If the person hides food, check hiding places regularly, and discreetly dispose of any perishable items.

Restlessness

What is it?
Some people with dementia experience general restlessness, which may show itself in pacing up and down and fidgeting.

What to say
'Come with me, I'll take you to the bathroom.'
'Do you want to go for a walk with me?'
'Would you like a cup of tea?'
'Would you like to go somewhere quiet?'

Possible causes
- The person may want to use the toilet but is unable to tell you.
- If a person has always been active and walked regularly, they may be missing this or want some fresh air.
- It could be a sign of hunger, thirst, constipation or pain, or the person may be ill or suffering from the side effects of medication.
- Other possibilities are boredom, anger, distress or anxiety, stress due to noisy or busy surroundings, or lack of exercise. It may also be due to changes that have taken place in the brain.

What to do

- Try asking the person whether they need to use the toilet, or lead them towards it. If they are adamant that they want to pace, try to find somewhere they can walk safely.
- Offer drinks and snacks.
- Check their feet regularly for redness, swellings or blisters, and try to persuade them to rest from time to time.
- Try to distract their attention and offer reassurance.
- Try giving the person something to occupy their hands, such as a soft toy or worry beads, or provide a 'rummage' box containing interesting objects.
- If the person seems upset, try to find the reason, give them some reassurance, then try to distract them with an interesting activity or by involving them in some form of exercise.

Suspicion

What is it?

Memory loss and disorientation can cause individuals with dementia to see situations in the wrong way. They may become suspicious of others – even those close to them – and accuse them of theft, infidelity or other offences.

What to say

'I'm sure you've put it somewhere. Let's look around.'

'I understand why you are upset. Let's go for a little walk/watch TV.'

Possible causes

Remember that the behaviour is caused by a disease that is affecting the person's brain.

What to do

- It is hurtful to be accused of something you did not do, but try not to be offended. Try to imagine what it would be like to continuously think your possessions are being taken or hidden (because you cannot remember where you put them).

- Do not try to argue with the person or convince them of your innocence. Instead, share a simple response with the person – for example, 'I see that you're upset that your purse is missing; I'll do my best to find it for you' – and avoid giving complicated explanations.

- Guide them to another activity to divert their attention.

Apathy

What is it?

Apathy is a lack of interest in or motivation to engage in activities. While apathy may not seem like a serious behaviour problem, it is not healthy for someone with dementia to simply sit around and do nothing, not showing interest in anything going on around them.

What to say

'Shall we look at your photo album? I haven't seen all of your photos.'

'What about watching the next episode of your programme? It was really exciting last time.'

(Use your suggesting and persuading phrases.)

Possible causes

Try to find out what may be triggering the apathy – for example, being ignored or becoming overwhelmed with a task. Another cause may be not having an appropriate choice of activities.

What to do

Even though the person is ill, it is important to keep them moving and as active as possible in order to maintain health and to prevent depression. Try simplifying activities they used to enjoy so the person can participate at a level that is comfortable and not too difficult. Even a small amount of activity is better than none at all.

Sundowning

What is it?

Sundowning is a term used to describe behaviours that get worse in the late afternoon and early evening – for example, increased confusion and agitation – and is most common with Alzheimer's disease.

What to say

Use your calming and reassuring phrases here.

Possible causes

It is not really understood why sundowning happens, but some think it is because the person is tired and as a result finds things more stressful, such as a busy, noisy dinnertime or a rushed bedtime routine. It also could be because of increasing confusion due to darkness and shadows.

What to do

The best way to approach sundowning is to make late afternoons and evenings as simple and relaxing as possible. Reduce distractions, unscheduled activities and behaviours that could be done at a different time of the day (e.g. switch to bathing in the morning) and keep rooms well lit until bedtime.

Wandering

What is it?

One of the most dangerous behaviours among people with dementia is wandering.

This may be:

- goal-directed – for example, the person thinks that they are going to a job or going 'home' to a childhood residence
- non-goal-directed – that is, the person wanders aimlessly.

What to say

'Come with me. Shall we look at your scrapbook?'

'It's too late/cold to go outside. Let's go and talk to Mary/play cards.'

Possible causes

People with dementia may forget where they are and wander as a result. Sometimes they decide to do something then get lost as they forget what it was they were going to do. Wandering may be the sign of distress or illness, or being unable to recognise familiar places. Side effects from medication can also be a cause.

What to do

To reduce the frequency of wandering, make sure the person has plenty of supervised activity to use up their energy.

English Check 7

1   Give a cause of trailing and checking.

_____

_____

2   Say what **not** to do when the person is being suspicious of you.

_____

_____

3   A lack of interest in everything is called _____

4   Give one example of what to do in cases of 'sundowning'.

_____

_____

5   What is thought to be one of the most dangerous behaviours of people with dementia?

_____

_____

6   What is a possible reason for hiding things?

_____

_____

7   Name a possible cause of restlessness and say what you would do about it.

_____

_____

Carer, look after yourself!

Caring can be a demanding and stressful job; even more so when caring for people with dementia. You may understand and agree with the theory of caring for this group of people but often the reality is more difficult, demanding and stressful than expected.

Feil and de Klerk-Rubin (2012) talk about 'centring' as one of the techniques for caring for people with dementia. Before you start work with each individual, take deep breaths in through the nose and expel through the mouth. Take two or three minutes so you can relax yourself before dealing with possibly difficult behaviour. Always remember that the person cannot help their behaviour.

Figure 4.2 Caring can be stressful

There is a lot of advice and support around for informal carers, someone caring for a loved one at home. However, the same guidelines are useful for the professional carer.

It is important as a caregiver to take care of yourself and to know the help and resources that are available to you. You also need to recognise if and when you are getting stressed.

Some of the signs of stress are:

- **anger and frustration** towards the person with dementia

- **depression** that affects your ability to cope

- **exhaustion** that makes it nearly impossible to complete necessary daily tasks

- **sleeplessness** caused by worrying about the situations and being able to cope

- **irritability** that leads to moodiness and triggers negative responses and actions – perhaps you snap back at people

- **lack of concentration** that makes it difficult to do everyday tasks.

What can you do?

- Get help. This can be from colleagues, your manager or support groups. If symptoms are very worrying then perhaps seek medical help.

- Do relaxation sessions. Find out what relaxes you and do regular sessions. Remember 'centring'.

- Physical exercise is highly recommended for stress. Getting outside to walk also provides relief.

- Make sure your diet is healthy.

Read more at:

www.alz.org/care/alzheimers-dementia-caregiver-stressburnout.asp#ixzz2Tp9vuJQR

Part 5

Encouraging conversation and activity
– What can I do?

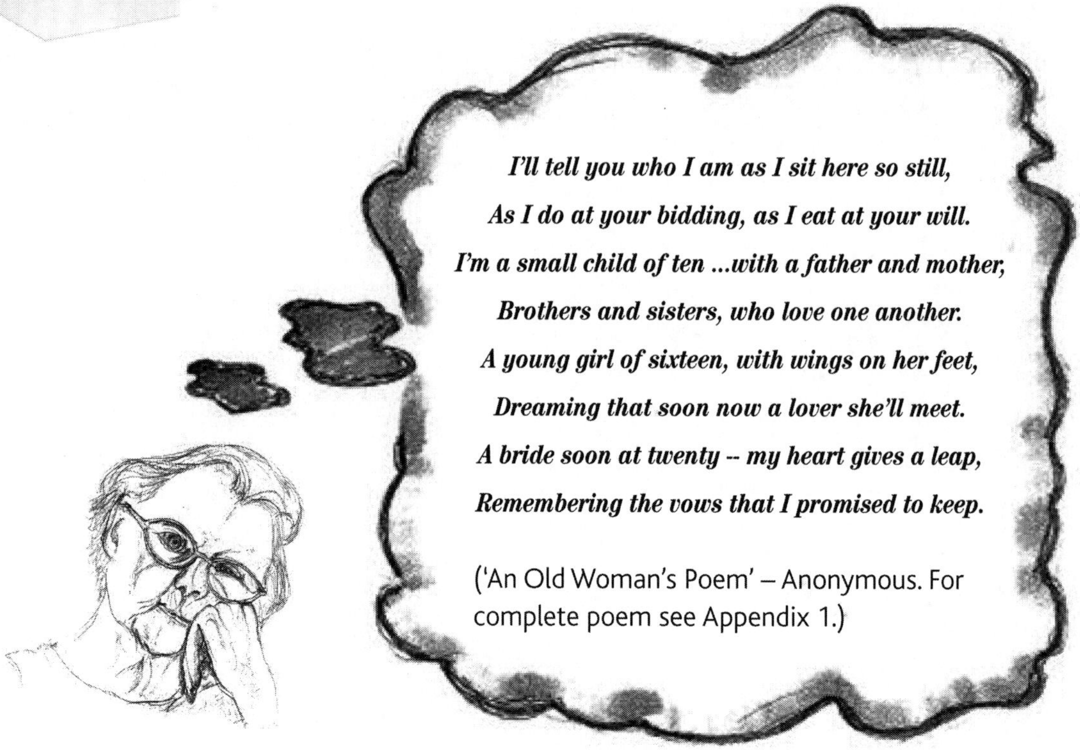

I'll tell you who I am as I sit here so still,
As I do at your bidding, as I eat at your will.
I'm a small child of ten ...with a father and mother,
Brothers and sisters, who love one another.
A young girl of sixteen, with wings on her feet,
Dreaming that soon now a lover she'll meet.
A bride soon at twenty -- my heart gives a leap,
Remembering the vows that I promised to keep.

('An Old Woman's Poem' – Anonymous. For
complete poem see Appendix 1.)

Figure 5.1 The thoughts of a person with dementia

Word Check 8

Check	✔	Meaning/translation
reminiscing		
accomplishments		
capabilities		
prompt		
appetite		
sleep patterns		
irritable		
self-assertive		
listless		
lethargy		
stickler		

We communicate for lots of reasons. We have looked at some specific reasons but we must not forget that we, as humans, communicate for pleasure. We communicate as a way of building relationships, developing friendships or just for the pleasure of socialising.

So communication should be used in this way for people with dementia. Of course, the depth and range of communication will depend on the stage of dementia. But as we have said previously, there is always some level of communication possible.

Remember! When communicating make sure you do the following.

- Be an active listener! Listen carefully to what is being said and respond accordingly.

- Check the environment. Is it quiet with no distractions?

- Check yourself. Are you physically in the right position for a conversation? Check eye level, and that you are sitting in front of the person, and so on. Are you showing positive body language?

- Check your voice is at the right level – loud enough but not too loud, calm and gentle.

- Check you have the attention of your listener.

Reminiscing

People with dementia can often remember the distant past more easily than recent events. If you can find a way to help them to remember these distant, pleasant memories, the person may become more lively and interested. Reminiscing not only exercises the brain, it also provides positive, pleasant feelings, which improve the quality of life.

The following points might be useful to consider when planning reminiscing.

Consider	
Time of day	When is the person most alert? Morning? Afternoon?
Comfortable location	Comfortable and free from distraction – no TV!
A table nearby	A nice cuppa always helps conversation!
Prompts/rummage box	Photographs, books with pictures, old household items, etc. These all help to raise interest.
A visit outside	This can prompt happy memories.

Table 5.1 Planning to reminisce

Warning!

Talking of the past can sometimes trigger unhappy memories. Be sensitive! But also remember that becoming emotional is not always a bad thing. Allow the person to express their feelings and be ready to comfort and support them.

So, how to start?

You'll probably have lots of ideas on questions – especially if you know the person quite well. However, you may not know anything about the person, so some questions are listed below to give you some ideas.

- What's the first home you remember as a child?
- Tell me about the jobs you did as a child to help your Mum.
- What was your favourite thing about school?
- Who was your best friend when you were a child?
- What was your favourite holiday activity?
- What did you want to be when you grew up?
- Who was your first boyfriend/girlfriend?
- Where did you meet your husband/wife and what was your first date like?
- What was your favourite toy?

You can find topics and questions for reminiscing on the Story Corps website: **http://storycorps.org/record-your-story/great-questions/list/**

Materials on the market

There is material available to help with this kind of activity. One excellent example is 'The Daily and Weekly Sparkle'.

The Daily Sparkle is a professionally written reminiscence and activity tool supported by some of UK's care organisations such as the NHS, Age UK and Dementia UK. It has a daily and weekly edition and is aimed at people in the early or mid-stages of dementia.

It is full of articles, quizzes, old news stories, gossip, puzzles, singalongs and entertainment geared towards stimulating the mind and improving memory. Each month there is an accompanying sing-a-long CD. They also give you a free training manual on how to organise reminiscing sessions.

The paper is aimed at getting people to reminisce and share experiences. There are also notes for the carer. Some examples are in Appendix 2.

More information is available at: **www.dailysparkle.co.uk**

Another excellent source of materials is the company Speechmark. They publish a wide range of materials for working with people with dementia. These include games and other activities to stimulate thinking, reminiscing and conversation.

An example of an activity for reminiscing is 'Life Histories Game' by Robin Dynes. There are several aims of the board game including helping to preserve memory, assisting with reminiscing and life histories, and providing opportunities for socialising and making friends.

Other materials include *The Reminiscence Quiz Book*, *The Reminiscence Puzzle Book*, reminiscing recipes and *The Memory Handbook*.

These and many more can be found on their website: **www.speechmark.net**

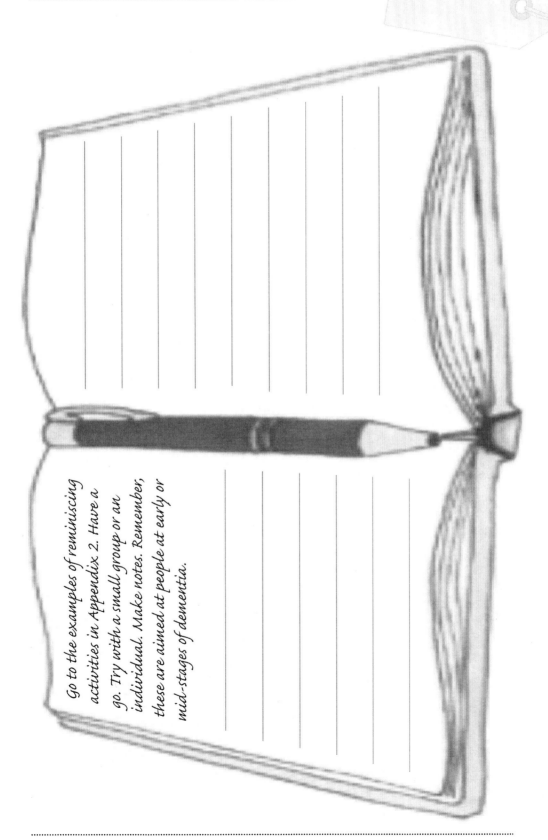

Go to the examples of reminiscing activities in Appendix 2. Have a go. Try with a small group or an individual. Make notes. Remember, these are aimed at people at early or mid-stages of dementia.

Life story/history

Linked closely to reminiscing is building up the person's life history. From this you can build up a personal life story book. This life history and information about their personality will also be useful when preparing the person-centred care plan. Therefore it is important to find out what the individual thinks and remembers.

Find time to sit down with the person and ask about their life. If they are able to tell you about this, you will learn a great deal and it will help you to develop a life story and history. To start, establish good two-way communication. Listen carefully to learn about their past before the onset of the disease. Knowing the background of the individual is important as their past experiences influence their current actions and behaviour.

What is a life history?

A person's past is a vital part of their dementia experience. Knowing about a person's history helps you to support the person with dementia today. It can provide information which might help identify certain behaviours.

A life history is more than just a series of life events. It includes:

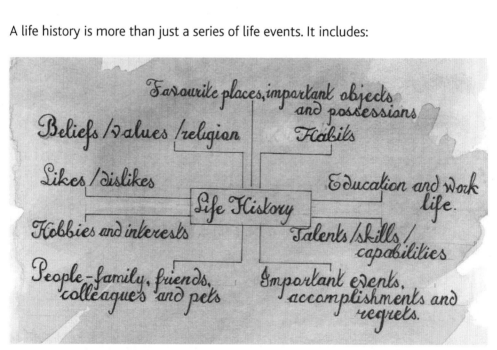

Figure 5.2 What is in a life history

How does life history help?

Knowing a person's past routines can be used now in their day-to-day care.

Families, friends and other carers may have a better chance of understanding what a person may be trying to communicate.

If you know the past – it can help to understand the present!

It can give clues to a person's strengths, what they are still capable of doing for themselves.

It can explain a person's current behaviour and actions and help to avoid triggers of difficult behaviour.

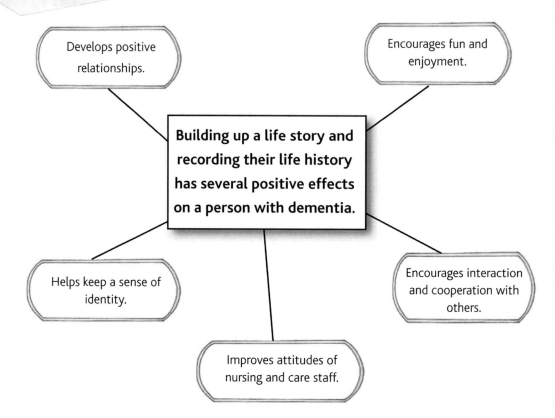

Develops positive relationships.

Encourages fun and enjoyment.

Building up a life story and recording their life history has several positive effects on a person with dementia.

Helps keep a sense of identity.

Encourages interaction and cooperation with others.

Improves attitudes of nursing and care staff.

How do I find out about the person's life history?

(See 'Reminiscing' above for points on how to 'set the scene'.)

Recent history is as valuable as past history but the person with dementia will probably be able to remember past events better.

However, to help to record present and recent details, The Alzheimer's Society has produced a template of a leaflet called 'This is me'. The aim is to give information which will help the carer to support the person with dementia. It can be filled in with the person, friends or family. The template is available at:
www.alzheimers.org.uk/thisisme

Collect the information in stages. A person with dementia may not be able to concentrate on one subject for very long.

Use prompts such as a particular time in their life or objects to trigger memories – see suggested questions in 'Reminiscing', above and rummage boxes.

How can I use life history?

- You can use the person's experiences to talk about the past, which they will probably find more interesting.

- Sometimes you can use their old habits and routines in how you care for them. Knowing how and when they used to do things can help to set up a more comfortable routine for them. It can also help to explain any difficult behaviour.

- The person may have a collection of old photographs that you could identify and label. This will allow you and others opportunities to chat about who is in a photo, where a photo was taken, holidays, places, pets, and so on.

- Sharing life history with younger family members or carers can make them see the person in a different way.
  http://www.dementiaweb.org.uk/life-history.php

You can help to write a 'Personal Life Story Book'!

If you put the person's life story into a book form it helps to keep the memories. Looking at past events helps to stimulate the memory and bring pleasure.

You can start with the leaflet 'This is me' (see above) and then develop it into a whole life story book.

Dementia UK and Central and North West London NHS Foundation Trust have developed a template to do just that and it is available at:
www.dementiauk.org/information-support/life-story-work

Also, *Writing Life Histories: a guide for use in caring environments* by Robin Dynes (2011) is a wonderful resource for helping to develop life histories. The book covers many aspects of writing and can be dipped into to help with whatever level you can go to with the person you are supporting.

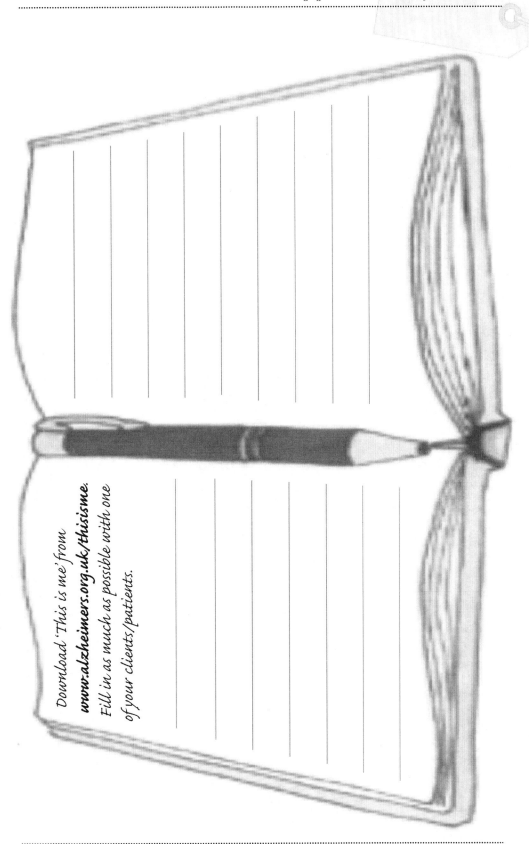

Download 'This is me' from *www.alzheimers.org.uk/thisisme*. Fill in as much as possible with one of your clients/patients.

Activities

There are currently many articles and views about activity and older people. In the past 10 years, research has shown that activities play a large part in preventing the progression of dementia. It is also known that socialising prevents loneliness, despair and suicidal thoughts.

The National Association for Providers of Activities for Older People (NAPA) have published a book, *The Good Practice Guide to Therapeutic Activities with Older People in Care Settings* (2005). In it they set out ideas, opinions and research.

They state that new thinking is as follows.

Meaningful activity is essential for maintaining physical and psychological well-being. Older people who disengage from activity through illness, disability or social isolation experience diminished health and well-being. Meaningful activity may be used therapeutically as an agent for positive change. (p.24)

The book lists many pieces of research going back to 1968, backing the positive benefits of activity in older people.

Some of the advantages are listed opposite plus what happens when activity is stopped for any reason.

Changes when activity is restarted after a period of inactivity	Changes when activity stops
Physical changes Muscle strength and joint mobility increase Bone loss decreases Blood pressure and threat of thrombosis lessens Appetite increases Bowel movements improve Continence improves Sleep improves **Psychological changes** Smiling, laughing and talking increase Social interaction increases Concentration and memory improve Less agitation and more relaxed Humour improves More self-assertive More affectionate	**Physical changes** Poor muscle and joints Bone loses calcium Blood pressure increases Appetite lessens Poor bowel activity Incontinence increases Pressure sores more prevalent Poor sleep patterns **Psychological changes** Less alert Poor concentration More irritable and impatient Listless and restless Depression and lethargy Problem-solving difficulties Confusion

Table 5.2 Advantages of activity. Based on NAPA (2005)

What is 'activity'?

When we talk of activities it is not just of a game of bingo, an outing or reminiscing, important though these are, it is about a whole range of activities. Anything where the person is involved in doing something; having a bath, writing a letter, laying the table are some examples.

Keeping busy stimulates the brains of people with dementia while boosting a sense of usefulness. But they lose the ability to choose good, appropriate activities and then to follow through on them – so you need to encourage and suggest things to do. Too much time doing nothing can make anyone feel lonely and useless, raising the risk of depression, agitation and anger.

Tips to make an activity a success for someone with dementia

- **Build on activities the person has always enjoyed.**

A bridge player may no longer be able to keep up, but they may enjoy holding cards and playing a simpler game. A chess player may no longer be able to play chess but could enjoy a simpler board game, like draughts. But introduce new ideas, too, to see what 'clicks'.

- **Aim for the right level – not too easy, not too hard.**

If an activity is too simple or childish (like colouring books for kids), the person might feel insulted or bored. If it requires remembering things or is too difficult for the person, it will frustrate and turn them off.

- **Take into account the fact that dementia progresses.**

The attention span shortens. Changes in recent memory make it hard to follow activities with lots of steps or instructions (such as cooking). Some people with dementia may be more able and successful at art. Consider music as musical ability tends to be very well retained.

- **Take mistakes or imperfection in your stride.**

Don't be a stickler for things being done the 'right' way or according to rules. If it bothers you that dishes are rinsed improperly, for example, redo them yourself later without comment. The main consideration should be how the activity makes the person feel: involved, purposeful, successful.

- **Be patient!**

Impatience or anger tends to make the person with dementia anxious. Don't give orders and make suggestions. Watch your body language, too: they notice cross faces and heavy sighs. What helps: **encouraging** comments and realistic **praise** (without talking down or using an exaggerated voice), saying thanks where appropriate.

- **Don't argue.**

Avoid asking 'Why?' when something goes wrong. People with dementia probably won't know why they did something peculiar (like store a paint set in the refrigerator). Gently suggest an alternative: 'I don't think the paint should get cold, so let's store it here on the desk.' Rational arguments are useless because the person's emotions are stronger than their logic.

- **Make activities routine.**

If an activity is a hit, do it every day or so. Or do the same thing, slightly modified: folding towels one day, sheets the next. Pursue categories of activities at about the same time every day (physical or outdoor in the morning, quiet handiwork after lunch) to add comforting structure to the day.

(Based on the article by Paula Spencer Scott from caring.com and available at: **www.caring.com/articles/activities-for-alzheimers-and-dementia**)

Possible areas of activity

There is a vast range of possible activities. You will have many ideas yourself. The following are some suggestions.

Area	Suggested activities
Self-care	Shower/bath, hair, nails, mending, shoe cleaning.
Creativity	Music, karaoke, art collage, gardening/tending plants, making a scrap book, photo collage, labelling old family photos.
Physical exercise	Seat exercises, dancing, skittles, bowls, playing catch with softball or beanbag, walking.
Sensory	Rummage bags, smell box, texture games, massage.
Daily living	Hand washing, ironing, looking after plants, dusting, tidying drawer/wardrobes, making drinks or snacks.
Puzzles and games	Easy crosswords and word searches that use large type. Jigsaw puzzles with very large pieces (not childish pictures!). Floor puzzles are good – large pieces and few of them. Work on these on a table so you don't have to struggle getting off the floor! Old favourites like dominoes, card games and board games. 'Life Histories' – a board game available through Speechmark (**www.speechmark.net**) which helps life histories and reminiscing, as well as encouraging socialising. Several games are available from Speechmark. Go to their website to see the list.

Area	Suggested activities
Sorting and organising	Coins, according to date, value or place of origin. The silverware drawer, rearranging the order of the forks, spoons and knives. Playing cards into decks that match, or into suits within a deck, or by numbers. Photos by topic, subject, type or date. Mix them up after you finish so they can be sorted in a different way next time. Sock drawer.
Reading activities	Read out loud or simply look through books and magazines that can lead to discussions. Reading *The Daily Sparkle*.

Table 5.3 Possible areas of activity

Resources

Remember, people with dementia can still derive enjoyment from activities they have always enjoyed. More ideas are available here:

- **www.caring.com/articles/activities-for-dementia-alzheimers-patients**

- **www.speechmark.net**

- NAPA (2005) *The Good Practice Guide to Therapeutic Activities with Older People in Care Settings*.

Keep up the communication!

Being involved in an activity gives you the opportunity to 'chat' with the person with dementia. Day-to-day small talk can be used. Just remember your basic points on communicating with people with dementia. You will get to know the person better and 'normality' is brought into the situation.

As you are doing the activity, you can:

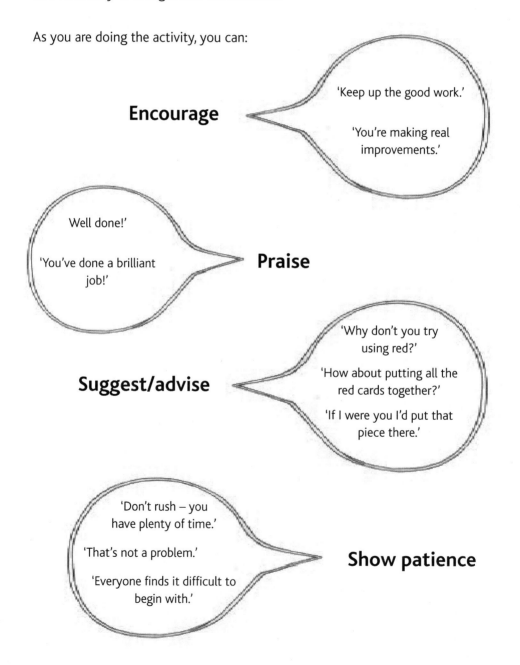

Encourage

'Keep up the good work.'

'You're making real improvements.'

Well done!'

'You've done a brilliant job!'

Praise

'Why don't you try using red?'

'How about putting all the red cards together?'

'If I were you I'd put that piece there.'

Suggest/advise

'Don't rush – you have plenty of time.'

'That's not a problem.'

'Everyone finds it difficult to begin with.'

Show patience

'Which shampoo do you like?'

'What colour nail varnish do you like?'

'When I was a child having shiny shoes was very important.'

'Did you used to do this as a child?'

'Who taught you how to do it?'

'I used to do this but I was never any good at it.'

Small talk/chatting

'Do you remember the rules to this game?'

'I played this as a child but used to cheat!!'

'You play this well. You must have had lots of practice.'

'I cut off crusts now but my mother always made me eat them.'

'What's your favourite sandwich filling?'

'Who's that in the photo?'

'Who is the eldest?'

'The dress looks really old fashioned now. I bet it was very fashionable then.'

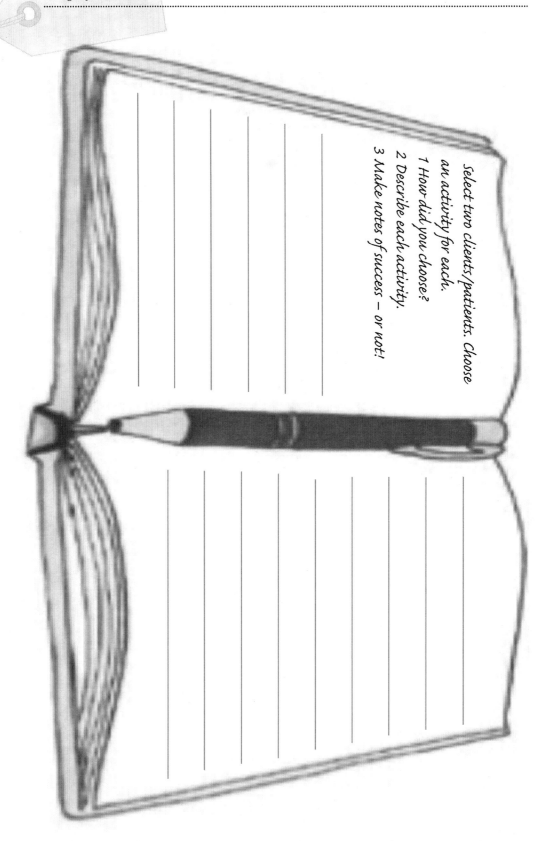

Select two clients/patients. Choose
an activity for each.
1 How did you choose?
2 Describe each activity.
3 Make notes of success – or not!

Conclusion

There is no doubting that the care of people with dementia is of massive importance and concern throughout the world. The government in the UK has given it top priority in the future of the NHS as well as in its policies on social care.

More and more, focus on the quality of care is gaining attention as thinking moves away from looking at the disease and moves towards looking at the quality of life of the person with dementia. The person-centred approach is well established as the recognised and accepted way of caring for people with dementia. Alongside this is the belief that communication is possible at some level and the carer must look beyond the dementia and see the person within.

> *It is possible to be involved in meaningful communication with the vast majority of people with dementia but we must be able to enter into their world, understand their sense of pace and time, recognise the problems of distraction and realise that there are many ways in which people express themselves and it is our responsibility to learn how to recognise these.*
>
> **(Goldsmith, 1996, p.165)**

At the forefront of all this is the care worker, who is:

- coping with the responsibilities of caring for elderly, vulnerable people
- adjusting to new ways of thinking
- coping with often extremely challenging behaviour
- often in a low-paid job with the stresses of staff shortages.

Without a doubt, to be a good carer under these circumstances certain qualities are needed:

- good communication skills
- patience, understanding, compassion

- a belief that communication with a person with dementia is always possible at some level

- dedication.

Most people would agree that it is time to recognise the work and dedication involved in the caring of vulnerable people and to give suitable recognition and status to the care worker.

Word Check

The English language is known to be a very rich language. One of the reasons for this is that many words have more than one meaning. In the list below only the meaning used in the text is explained.

abnormal Something is abnormal if it is different from what is usual. So the cells were abnormal – they were different from the usual cells, or the normal cells.

accommodate If you accommodate someone you do or provide what they want or need.

accomplishments These are impressive things that someone has done.

acknowledge To admit the existence, reality, or truth of someone or something. To acknowledge something or someone is to accept that something is true.

aggression This is when angry feelings or behaviour make someone want to attack other people – either physically or verbally.

agitation This is the feeling when someone is worried or disturbed and may show in overactivity or nervousness.

anxious If someone is anxious they are worried and afraid or troubled about something.

apathetic If someone is apathetic they are not interested in anything, or not concerned about things that are happening around them.

apathy The name of the feeling; apathetic is the adjective which describes this feeling.

appetite Appetite is wanting food. A healthy/good appetite means the person wants to eat and feels hungry. A poor appetite is when they do not want to eat or don't feel hungry.

approaches	Approaches are the ways that something (usually a problem), is dealt with. 'How shall we approach this problem?'
appropriate	If something is appropriate it is suitable or right for the situation.
belittle	If you belittle someone you say something to make them feel unimportant or not very good.
capabilities	Your capabilities are the things you are able to do.
compassion	If you show compassion you show sympathy or pity to someone who is suffering.
concepts	These are general ideas about something. The concept or ideas of equality are necessary in the person-centred approach to care.
concern	If you show concern, are concerned about someone, it means you are worried or anxious about them.
confused	If someone is confused it means they cannot think clearly and get things mixed up.
criticise	If you criticise someone you find fault with something they have said or done.
dignity	To have dignity is to be calm and serious and so earn respect.
disorientated	If you are disorientated you are confused and don't know where you are.
empathise	If you empathise with someone you can imagine how they are feeling and so understand how they are acting.
encouragement	If you give encouragement to someone you give them hope, support or confidence to do something.

fidget	If someone fidgets they move about or play with something in a restless way, usually because they are bored, nervous or generally restless.
flexibility	Having flexibility is about being able to change when the situation changes.
frustrated	When you are frustrated it means you feel angry or dissatisfied because you cannot do something or have something you want.
functions	The function of something is the purpose of it, what it is for. The brain has many functions or purposes.
genetic	If something is genetic it is linked to genes, that is it is passed from parents to children.
gesture	This is a movement of the hand or head, and so on, that has a meaning. For example, a shake of the head means no, a wave of the hand means goodbye.
hallucinations	If you have hallucinations you see or hear something that is not there.
humiliate	If you humiliate someone you make them feel ashamed, usually in front of other people.
inhibitions	If you have inhibitions it means you don't express your feelings easily or you are not relaxed. To have no inhibitions means the opposite and you act or speak without restrictions, often inappropriately.
intensify	To intensify something is to make it greater or stronger.
irritable	If someone is irritable, they are easily made angry.
lethargy	This is the feeling of being tired and having no energy, not wanting to do anything.

listless
Very similar meaning to lethargic – being tired, without energy.

memory
Your ability to remember things. 'She has a poor memory, she can't remember what she did last week.'

model
A model is an example of how something is done, usually so that it can be copied. So, the social model of dementia shows what is done if you view dementia this way.

mood
This is how you feel. You can be in a good mood, therefore happy, or a bad mood, angry and/or miserable.

mumble
If you mumble you speak quietly without opening your mouth properly so people find it difficult to hear you.

optimism
This is a feeling you have when you think the future will be good or successful. You feel optimistic about it.

out of the blue
If something happens 'out of the blue' it is sudden and unexpected.

pace
When someone paces they walk with regular steps up and down a room/area, often without purpose or having nowhere to go.

personality
Your personality describes the type of person you are, your features, your qualities. 'Joe has a strong personality', 'Alice has an outgoing personality.'

persuade
To try to get someone to do something by giving them a good reason to do it.

posture
This is the way you sit or stand, how you hold your body.

praise
If you praise someone you say how good they are, or how good something they have done is if it deserves to be admired.

priorities	Things placed in order of how important they are to you. 'My top priority is not to be ignored.'
prompt, to	To help someone to continue speaking, or to remember something, by giving them a reminder. Old photographs can often prompt pleasant memories.
reasoning	Forming judgements or opinions after thinking about something in a logical way.
reassure	To say or do something to make somebody feel less frightened, worried or nervous. You give reassurance.
reminiscing	To reminisce is to talk about pleasant things that have happened in the past.
repetitive behaviour	Repetitive actions are actions repeated over and over again, so becoming annoying to people watching the behaviour.
rights	Your rights are what you are allowed to do by law. In Britain everyone has the right to vote at 18. They also include how you are treated. There is a list of basic human rights, for example, the right to privacy, the right not to be discriminated against.
risk	There is a risk if there is a possibility of something dangerous or unpleasant happening.
self-assertive	You say things clearly and firmly about what you think.
self-esteem	You have self-esteem when you think well of yourself.
sensitive	If you are sensitive to someone you understand their feelings and/or their problems.
sincere	If you are sincere you really mean what you say and are not pretending; you are honest.

sleep patterns A sleep pattern is how you sleep; perhaps you sleep all night, perhaps you keep waking up, perhaps you find it difficult to fall asleep but then sleep well.

spherical Shaped like a ball.

stickler A stickler is someone who insists on sticking closely to the rules or format.

stroke, a A stroke is a serious medical condition that occurs when the blood supply to part of the brain is cut off.

suggest To put forward an idea or a plan that people will discuss and decide upon. 'Tom suggested a game of cards.'

sundowning A 'new' word given to the way behaviour worsens in the early evening with people with dementia. For example, increased confusion and agitation.

suspicion This is a feeling that something is wrong or somebody has done something wrong. 'She treated everyone with suspicion, even her family.'

symptoms These are signs of illness. Sneezing is a symptom of a cold. Memory loss is a symptom of dementia.

tackle To deal with a problem in a strong way. 'We must tackle this problem of security before someone gets hurt.'

tangles Confused masses of hair, threads, and so on. For example, hair can get tangled in your comb, string can get tangled and become difficult to untangle. Tangles in the brain are a sign of Alzheimer's disease.

trailing and checking To trail someone is to follow them or walk behind them. Checking is to make sure something is correct or it is there. Trailing and checking is a behaviour associated with dementia.

triggers   A trigger causes something to happen or start.

unique   Something unique is different from everything else, the only one of its type.

valued, to be   To be valued is to be thought of as useful and important.

verbally   A verbal message is a message that is spoken, not written. So we can say 'A message that is spoken, not written, is "made verbally".'

wandering   To wander is to move from place to place without purpose. This term 'wandering' has been used to describe a behaviour of people with dementia.

Add your own words below:

_____   _____

_____   _____

_____   _____

_____   _____

_____   _____

_____   _____

_____   _____

_____   _____

_____   _____

_____   _____

_____   _____

_____   _____

_____   _____

Appendix 1

An Old Woman's Poem, Anonymous

An old woman died in the geriatric ward of a small hospital near Dundee, Scotland. It was thought she had nothing of value in her possessions. Later, when the nurses were going through her belongings, they found this poem. They were so moved and impressed that it was photocopied and a copy given to every nurse in the hospital. It is now available all over the Web and forms part of many training courses in care homes and hospitals.

How moving to think this woman, thought to have nothing of value, is the author of this beautiful, eloquent poem which has travelled the world by Internet and influenced so many people to look at the elderly with fresh eyes!

An Old Woman's Poem

What do you see, nurses, what do you see?
What are you thinking when you're looking at me?
A crabby old woman, not very wise,
Uncertain of habit, with faraway eyes?
Who dribbles her food and makes no reply
When you say in a loud voice, 'I do wish you'd try!'
Who seems not to notice the things that you do,
And forever is losing a stocking or shoe …
Who, resisting or not, lets you do as you will,
With bathing and feeding, the long day to fill …
Is that what you're thinking? Is that what you see?
Then open your eyes, nurse; you're not looking at me.

I'll tell you who I am as I sit here so still,
As I do at your bidding, as I eat at your will.
I'm a small child of ten … with a father and mother,
Brothers and sisters, who love one another.
A young girl of sixteen, with wings on her feet,

Dreaming that soon now a lover she'll meet.
A bride soon at twenty – my heart gives a leap,
Remembering the vows that I promised to keep.
At twenty-five now, I have young of my own,
Who need me to guide and a secure happy home.
A woman of thirty, my young now grown fast,
Bound to each other with ties that should last.
At forty, my young sons have grown and are gone,
But my man's beside me to see I don't mourn.
At fifty once more, babies play round my knee,
Again we know children, my loved one and me.
Dark days are upon me, my husband is dead;
I look at the future, I shudder with dread.
For my young are all rearing young of their own,
And I think of the years and the love that I've known.

I'm now an old woman ... and nature is cruel;
'Tis jest to make old age look like a fool.
The body, it crumbles, grace and vigour depart,
There is now a stone where I once had a heart.
But inside this old carcass a young girl still dwells,
And now and again my battered heart swells.
I remember the joys, I remember the pain,
And I'm loving and living life over again.
I think of the years ... all too few, gone too fast,
And accept the stark fact that nothing can last.

So open your eyes, nurses, open and see,
... Not a crabby old woman; look closer ... see ME!!

(Anonymous)

Appendix 2

Daily and Weekly Sparkle Examples

THE WAY WE WERE

I wonder how many housewives of our generation had a 'Baking Day'? For me, it tended to be towards the end of the week. I liked to get the washing and ironing out of the way on Monday and Tuesday. Wednesday was a good cleaning day, so baking was usually on a Thursday or Friday. It also meant we had something in the cake tin at the weekend.

Sometimes I saved the trimmings from pastries and pies, so that the girls could make jam tarts when they came home from school. The whole house smelled of baking when Stan got home from work.

THE WAY WE WERE

One of the first things I had in my 'bottom drawer' was a lovely blue and white 'Cornish Ware' jug. One of my friends brought it back from her holiday in Falmouth. Those blue and white stripes always reminded me of the seaside.

Cornish Ware was made by T.G. Green at their factory in Derbyshire, but the clay came from Cornwall. We added to our collection that started with the jug. We used the familiar blue-ringed bowls and plates and cups and saucers at breakfast time every day for years. Cathie has still got some of them.

DO YOU REMEMBER?

I was having a clear out the other day and found this Dinky toy bus. You can see for yourself that it was well used. I don't remember when and where I got it – but I know it was at the seaside. We had gone on an outing in a bus just like this. I can remember being almost in tears because I wanted to sit in the high-up bit at the back but all those seats were taken when we got on.

As we walked down the sea front we saw this one in a shop window and Dad – bless him – went in and bought it for me. He and Ma also got us back to the coach early so that we were first on and got high-up seats. It's the little things like that which make parents great!

DO YOU REMEMBER?

I loved to have my Fish & Chips wrapped in newspaper. This isn't allowed now but when I was a teenager that's what they were always wrapped in. I used to wait for the mobile Fish & Chip van every Friday. Under my arm would be a bundle of the past week's newspapers which we had collected for Mr. Cyril who owned the van.

In return he always gave me an extra big portion of chips with my fish. The newspaper always seemed to make them taste better – and I could catch up on the sports news in the papers that we hadn't bought as well! Now that's what I call real recycling!

WHO INVENTED IT?

Name the inventors of these useful objects.

1. Telephone.
James Watt or *Alexander Graham Bell*

2. Lightbulb.
Humphry Davy or *Thomas Edison*

3. Radio.
Marconi or *Logie Baird*

4. Fountain pen.
Lewis Waterman or *William Shakespeare*

5. Printing Press.
William Caxton or *Geoffrey Chaucer*

ANSWERS

5. *William Caxton*
4. *Lewis Waterman*
3. *Marconi*
2. *Thomas Edison*
1. *Alexander Graham Bell*

THE YELLOW BRICK ROAD

We're off to see the ----,
The Wonderful Wizard of ----.
You'll find he is a whiz of a Wiz
If ever a ---- there was.
If ever oh ever a Wiz there was
The Wizard of Oz is one ----,
Because, because, because, because, because.
Because of the wonderful things he ----.
We're ---- to see the Wizard.
The Wonderful Wizard of Oz.

---- the Yellow Brick Road.
Follow the ---- Brick Road.
Follow, follow, follow, follow,
Follow the Yellow Brick ----.

ANSWERS

9. *Road* 8. *Yellow* 7. *Follow*
6. *off* 5. *does* 4. *because*
3. *Wiz* 2. *Oz* 1. *Wizard*

(Reproduced by kind permission of 'The Daily and Weekly Sparkle')

Carers' notes

The way we were

1 Baking day

Background: Some housewives were quite systematic about doing certain tasks on certain days. Others were happy to do jobs like baking as and when it was needed. Sometimes they would make use of the oven if it was switched on for making other things – for example, stews or other items cooked in the oven.

Questions: When did you do baking? How did you decide which day to do housework and household chores? Did anyone else help? What things did you like to bake?

Cornish Ware

Background: This familiar blue and white striped pottery was one of the most often seen designs on British tables. It went a bit out of fashion in the 1960s but has experienced a renewed popularity more recently.

Questions: Do you like Cornish Ware? What does the blue and white stripe design remind you of? What items of crockery did you have in Cornish Ware?

Do you remember?

1 Dinky toy buses

Background: This is a typical toy from Dinky. It is a model of what was called an 'observation coach'. These road coaches copied the classic American railways' 'observation cars'. They were made by a firm called Whitson between 1949 and 1952 who used chassis made by different companies.

Questions: Did you have trips to the seaside? Which seaside places did you like best? Did you have Dinky toys to play with? Did you have a favourite one?

2 Fish and chips in newspaper
Background: The practice of wrapping fish and chips in newspaper lasted through

to the late 1970s. It was banned in case people got poisoned by the ink then being used on newsprint. Many felt that the paper actually gave the fish and chips a better smell and taste, and kept it warm and moist until they got home!

Questions: Do you like fish and chips? Do you remember it being wrapped in newspaper? Did you have a mobile chippy come round during the week? Which fried fish do you like best (cod, plaice, haddock, rock, etc)?

English Check – Answers

English Check 1

1 symptom   2 functions   3 frustrated   4 empathise   5 stroke

6 apathetic

English Check 2

1 differences   2 opportunities   3 person-centred   4 Own words but include some of following – how seen by others, dignity, respect, see person not dementia

English Check 3

Your own words here – examples/suggestions:

1 Hello Mary, you look upset. What's the matter?
   Do you want me to look at it? Show me where it's hurting? Did you knock it?

2 Hi Harry, you seem angry about something. What is it?
   What kind of dog is it? Does it usually do any damage? I'm sure your neighbour will come and get it soon. Let's go for a nice cuppa.

English Check 4

Your own words here – examples/ suggestions:

1 What's the matter Anne, you look very upset?
   I'm really sorry to hear that, Anne, you must be very disappointed. Do you want me to help you write a get well card?

2 Hi Hilda, What's upsetting you?
   Let me have a look. I think it's just the wind making that branch tap the window, but I can see why you are frightened, it just sounds like banging.

English Check 5

1 don't we   2 go out   3 tidying your room   4 don't you   5 Let's go

6 about asking   7 about going

English Check 6

Your own words here – examples/ suggestions:

1 Come on Christine, take your time, you can do it.
  Well done, I told you you could do it.

2 You're right Henry, it is a bit chilly. Why don't you put your thick, blue sweater on.

3 Hi Thomas, you look fed up, what's the matter?

  Oh dear, having one of those days? Let's see if we can cheer you up. What about a game of cards?

English Check 7

1 Feeling insecure and anxious. Only feeling safe when someone is near.

2 Don't be offended. Don't argue.

3 Apathy.

4 Make late afternoon relaxing, reduce distractions, do activities earlier in the day.

5 Wandering.

6 Insecurity, wanting to hold on to what they have left.

7 Toilet – take them there / Want to walk – take them out / Hunger, thirst – offer them something/ Boredom – organise an activity, etc.

You have a go 1 and 2

Your own words here. **Remember!** The situations are real for the person. Accept the situation. Don't argue. Calm, reassure and comfort.

References

Alzheimers Association. *Early Onset Dementia: a national challenge, a future crisis*; 2006. Available at:
www.alz.org/national/documents/report_earlyonset_summary.pdf

Alzheimer's Society. *Communication: best ways to interact with a person with dementia*. Available at:
www.alz.org/national/documents/brochure_communication.pdf

Alzheimer's Society. *Caregiver Stress*. Available at: **www.alz.org/care/alzheimers-dementia-caregiver-stress-burnout.asp#ixzz2Tp9vuJQR**

Alzheimer's Society. *Dealing with Aggressive Behaviour*. Available at:
www.alzheimers.org.uk/site/scripts/documents_info.php?documentID=96

Alzheimer's Society. *The Later Stages of Dementia*. Available at:
www.alzheimers.org.uk/site/scripts/documents_info.php?documentID=101

Alzheimer's Society. *Statistics*. Available at: **www.alzheimers.org.uk/statistics**

Alzheimer's Society. *This is me*. Available at:
www.alzheimers.org.uk/site/scripts/documents_info.php?documentID=1290

Alzheimer's Society. *Dementia and Aggressive Behaviour*. Available at
http://www.alzheimers.org.uk/site/scripts/documents_info.php?documentID=96

Alzheimer's Society. *Unusual Behaviour*. Available at:
www.alzheimers.org.uk/site/scripts/documents.php?categoryID=200357

Better Health Channel. *Dementia: communication issues*. Available at:
www.betterhealth.vic.gov.au

Bryden C. *Who Will I Be When I Die?* London: Jessica Kingsley Publishers; 2012.

Care UK. *Factsheet – Person-Centred Planning*. Available at:
www.careuklearningdisabilities.com/uploads/pdf/Factsheet_person_centred_planning.pdf

Caring.com. *Activities for Alzheimer's and Dementia Patients*. Available at: **www.caring.com/articles/activities-for-dementia-alzheimers-patients**

Daily and Weekly Sparkle. Available at: **www.dailysparkle.co.uk**
http://www.caring.com/about/caring_images.html

De Bellis A, Bradley SL, Wotherspoon A, *et al. Come Into My World – How to Interact with a Person who has Dementia: an educational resource for undergraduate healthcare students on person-centred care.* Flinders University, Adelaide: Hyde Park Press; 2009. Available at: **http://nursing.flinders.edu.au/comeintomyworld**

Dementia UK. *Life Story Work*. Available at **www.dementiauk.org/information-support/life-story-work**

Dementia Web. *Life History Factsheet*. Available at: **www.dementiaweb.org.uk/life-history.php**

Department of Health. UK to use G8 to target global effort on dementia; May 2013. Available at: **www.gov.uk/government/news/uk-to-use-g8-to-target-global-effort-on-dementia**

Dynes R. *Writing Life Histories: a guide for use in caring environments*. Milton Keynes: Speechmark; 2011.

Dynes R. *Life Histories Game*. Milton Keynes: Speechmark; 2012

Epp TD. Person-centred dementia care: a vision to be refined. *The Canadian Alzheimer's Disease Review*. April 2003: 14–18. Available at: **www.stacommunications.com/customcomm/Back-issue_pages/AD_Review/adPDFs/april03e/14.pdf**

Family Caregiver Alliance. *Caregiver's Guide to Understanding Dementia Behaviors.* Available at: **www.caregiver.org/caregiver/jsp/content_node.jsp?nodeid=391**

Feil N, De Klerk-Rubin V. *The Validation Breakthrough*. 3rd ed. Baltimore; 2012.

Genova L. *Still Alice*. London: Simon & Schuster UK Ltd; 2009.

Goldsmith M. *Hearing the Voice of People with Dementia: opportunities and obstacles*. London: Jessica Kingsley Publishers; 1996.

i newspaper. Elderly patients will get personal NHS worker to coordinate health care, pledges Jeremy Hunt; 13 May 2013.

NAPA. *The Good Practice Guide to Therapeutic Activities with Older People in Care Settings*. Milton Keynes: Speechmark; 2005.

Steckl C. *Tips for Dealing with Specific Dementia Problematic Behaviours*. Staats Reiss N, editor. Available at:
www.gulfbend.org/poc/view_doc.php?type=doc&id=15346.

Spencer Scott P. *How to Keep Someone With Alzheimer's or Other Dementias Busy and Active*. Available at: **www.caring.com/articles/activities-for-alzheimers-and-dementia**

Stokes G. *And Still the Music Plays*. 2nd ed. London: Hawker Publication Ltd; 2010.

Storycorps. Available at: **http://storycorps.org/record-your-story/great-questions/list/**

Tan R. *Dementia Awareness in CALD Communities across the Generations. An Australian Government Initiative*. East Melbourne: Migrant Information Centre; 2010. Available at:
www.miceastmelb.com.au/documents/Dementia/DementiaAwarenessProjectReport.pdf

CPD with Radcliffe

You can now use a selection of our books to achieve CPD (Continuing Professional Development) points through directed reading.

We provide a free online form and downloadable certificate for your appraisal portfolio. Look for the CPD logo and register with us at: **www.radcliffehealth.com/cpd**